Come to the Garden

Christy Sawyer

This book is dedicated to all my
wonderful "River Dwellers", and also to
the team of ladies God gave me to help
birth and lead this amazing ministry
opportunity that impacts women all over
Southwest Florida . . . and beyond.

Come to the Garden
© 2018 by Christy Sawyer

Printed in the United States of America
Cover layout and title design: Alex Macpherson, Macpherson Designs
Interior Layout: Robert W. Ahrens, Inspired Media Productions

CONTENTS

Introduction

My first invitation to *"COME TO THE GARDEN"* was offered by Christy Sawyer, one of my favorite women of power and influence for Christ.

Christy was relating her life story to our congregation as part of her message. Here's why it matters:

I was riveted by Christy's compelling words of declared triumph and success as a Christian business woman and her ministry alongside husband, Jonathan, our Minister of Music. Yet I was stunned by her narratives of her earlier past personal failures which had preceded the current marvelous season of Christy's exemplary life. Her humility and vulnerability in openly sharing her pain and brokenness moved my heart deeply. All I had seen was the result of her journey out of brokenness into the "Christ-in-you" glory (Col. 1:27). I had only seen her restored glory in action, the present glory of the woman God had originally created her to become!

Christy was amazing that night! As a dynamic and gifted speaker and teacher, she was powerfully anointed, speaking words of hope and comfort while offering the ministry of the Holy Spirit to everyone with any need. She was proof of God's power to give hope, to help, to heal and restore. She stood there as a living testimony of God's transforming work by the Holy Spirit, inviting us to come to the Lord in full surrender, to allow Him to take control if we would fully yield to Him, to learn to live from the fullness of His Presence. She invited us to intimacy in our walk with God's Presence daily— our "ever-present help in time of need!"

When Christy asked me to write the forward to her book, this night came to mind. I realized that Christy's offer of restoration to wholeness was actually a preliminary moment of revelation to me of her testimony to God's desire to restore us to original wholeness,

Garden of Eden fellowship, and His Spirit-to-spirit walk with us. How could I have missed this all these years? Christy made it so clear!

God's love for all people everywhere requires they hear of how this can be. God is still after fellowship with all people everywhere . . . that intimacy of union Spirit-to-Spirit which can only be possible if we are restored to Life through faith in Jesus Christ as the Holy Spirit draws us to the redeeming and reconciling grace of God! Somebody has to tell people. Everybody has a right to know! Christy is making disciples who are telling people, women specifically, about God's desire for His love to flood their whole life!

From the beginning, God's invitation to have "Garden of Eden" intimacy with Him has been His original design and plan. God's Genesis account in the opening pages of the Bible describes His hand-made creation of Adam and Eve for Garden living. It was there, in God's exquisite garden beauty, where they literally walked with God face-to-face in perfect harmony, freely enjoying God's company. They experienced wholeness and completeness in His Presence, their daily experience. Adam and Eve enjoyed a perfect union with God Himself in His Garden, a perfect place prepared for God's beloved human beings.

The simplest version of God's creation of us humans, the crowning glory of His creation, is that He made us with His own hands. All other creation was by His spoken word as in "God-said-and-it-was-so" creation days.

The Bible teaches that we humans are uniquely hand-made in God's original design and in God's image with the capacity for spirit-to-Spirit fellowship and communion with God. Although we have no promise of a physical Garden of Eden being restored until God's new earth, we do have God's desire for us to enjoy His Presence within, this same "walk in the Spirit" relationship with Him. Through faith in Jesus Christ, the Holy Spirit imparts His Life to us! God's restores spiritual pleasures for our daily living.

Hearing Christy's life story has given me such renewed hope for everyone, but especially women, regardless of brokenness and pain, whether due to our sin and its resultant shame or that of others who have harmed us. Out of the chaos and void in our lives, God creates "Garden of Eden delights" as in Christy's life. Her personal stories illustrate the power of God's Word. Her restored life proves the power of the Holy Spirit to make Christ-likeness an expectation for everyone. Her message leads you into the "garden" of God's promised "Eden restoration" (Isaiah 51:3 " . . . her wilderness He will make like Eden, and her desert like the garden of the LORD"). The Holy Spirit will take us into the fullness of His Presence using her testimony of life experience in trusting God's faithfulness to biblical promises.

It was Christy's early draft of this book which so beautifully led me into the Word, inviting me to allow the Holy Spirit to restore the sweet awareness of His Presence. I was able to allow God's favor and blessings to abound, replacing the weariness of wasted moments lesser "gods" had been allowed to occupy. How subtly deception was working to crush my trust in the pristine purity of my Savior's life within, the Spirit of Life in Christ Jesus and His abiding Presence within me.

As I turned to Christ in true repentance, changing my focus to see His Presence filling my being, He restored what had slipped from my grip – my trust in God Himself, my only reliable strength and wisdom. In the weariness of daily responsibilities while caring for my husband during recovery from open-heart surgery, I was trusting in my own strength (I was getting weak physically) and leaning to my own limited understanding (see Proverbs 3:5,6). God was waiting to be acknowledged as my ONLY Source of Spirit-Life and strength, living fully in Him. So beautifully God restores strength as I acknowledge His continual abiding Presence. He is always our "greater-than" GOD!

How beautifully God is growing Christy's influence in discipling women to reaching women and families for Christ! We are seeing almost explosive growth of her live-weekly River Dwellers discipleship sessions for women hungry for God. We all see the dynamic results and eternal worth of her expanding personal ministry. *These can be found at facebook.com/christysawyerministries.*

Our marvelous sanctuary choir has the privilege of Christy's anointed teaching and Godly wisdom from the Word in their Sunday Bible class. This is powerful preparation for Pastor Jonathan and the musicians and choir leading anointed worship with the full congregation gathering to enter into God's Presence to praise and worship and then the ministry of the anointed Word through God's servant.

Christy is part of a dynamic duo for God. She works alongside her husband Jonathan, leading the music ministry in our campus services and classes. Their scope of ministry includes a Creative Arts Academy and TV and Media Ministries needing music - you begin to see the dimension of their influence locally and globally. We are blessed to have their influence on our personal lives and ministries day by day while God is expanding their influence to reach the nations for Christ. Christy's retreats and her books are also ways God is expanding her discipleship training for women here and through media.

Christy's teaching at the "Come to the Garden Retreat" produced dynamic accounts of Christy allowing the fragrance of His Presence to permeate the retreat atmosphere. Women wanted to again be present in a retreat setting to experience God's Spirit-overflow as Christy taught His Word. They wanted to feel God's Spirit changing them and hear transformed women telling what God is doing in their lives as they seek the Lord together. Retreat is a place you are sure to find the way to God's hope and help and healing and wholeness.

I love conversations with Christy. She has a powerful "Life-livingness" to her conversations. She radiates joy ... a joy only found in God Himself. You can feel her desire to stir your heart to allow God to enable your own breakthrough in union and communion with Him overflowing to bless others. She creates hunger for God to work through your life in reaching others with the Gospel of Jesus Christ.

My own daily worship focus has been restored by reading *Come to the Garden*. It is the intensity of Christy's focus on the power of the Holy Spirit which convinces you of God's desire to create in you a conscious awareness of His Presence. The Word of God in Christy's mouth declares God's intent to restore Eden's blessings to replace what has been lost! Even though Satan uses "Last Days deception" by lesser gods, clothed in enticing brilliance, to entangle our faulty affections, God is restoring all that has been lost or stolen by the enemy. I find that God used Christy's words to restore me from spiritual dullness to vivid awareness of God's Presence – a fresh working of the Holy Spirit!!

The message of this book is clearly the Holy Spirit speaking through Christy words and personality as she expresses God's invitation to live in the triumph of restored daily fellowship and worship in His Presence. In Him we may enjoy the full delights and fulfillment living in the fullness of God's Spirit-Presence. Christy invites you to "Come to the Garden!"

This book may be your companion, along with your Bible, to sustain fellowship as you walk in harmony with God's Presence. His delight is that you enjoy Him as His beloved in His Garden of delights offered in His Word, the Bible. You'll soon begin to tell your own story of His transforming Presence, leading others to Him!

I recommend you cling to Christy's words from His Word ... they are Spirit and Life!

Darlene Betzer
Fort Myers, FL

Introduction
The Dream

"The walk of faith is to live according to the revelation we have received, in the midst of the mysteries we can't explain."

— Bill Johnson

I had a dream. I had this dream in 2010. I dreamt I pulled into the driveway of my place of business. (In reality, I owned a historic Victorian house that housed my business.) On with the dream — I pulled into the driveway and felt disgust and despair. I got out of the car and really wanted to get back in, drive away, and never come back. The yard was a mess. There was nothing growing, nothing green. Everything was dead. In real life, I was continuously frustrated because I could never get grass to grow there as a result of the giant magnolia tree in the center of the yard that shed leaves terribly. There were sticks and limbs and rotted leaves and stones, debris and dead things everywhere. I reached down to pick up a stick and thought to myself, "What's the point? There are thousands more."

I felt so overwhelmed. I went into the old house so I wouldn't have to look at it anymore. When I came back out, I was stunned! I was overjoyed! I felt like I had a new lease on life! Although the ground was still brown, although there was nothing green, although there was nothing growing, all the debris, all the dead things, had been removed. There was no life, but there was order. I cried out to God in delight, "Thank you, thank you, thank you!" I was so relieved. And God spoke to me (not sure how to explain how He spoke, because it wasn't really an audible voice), "Christy," I imagined Him shaking His head in slight irritation, "you are excited because I cleaned up your mess. You have no idea the plans I have for you, and they go way beyond Me just cleaning up your mess." I heard Him, but all I could take in at that moment was that He had removed all that was keeping me down. My burden had been lifted.

In part two of the dream, I pulled into the driveway a second time on a different day. The yard was still brown, but it was still clean! I was still filled with joy. There are two flowerbeds that are made with stones that go around two trees in the yard. Of course, in real life, nothing grew in them because of the magnolia leaves. As I walked closer to the yard, I noticed something different about those beds. What? There were tiny green shoots coming up, and, not only that, there were tiny purple and yellow blooms growing! I wanted to do cartwheels across the yard and into the street! I said, "My God, my God! Thank You, thank You, thank You! Not only did you clean up my mess, but now there is life here!" Small as it was, it was absolutely thrilling to me. I felt like I could've died right there, and I would have died happier than I've ever been. And God said, "Little girl," — He calls me that sometimes — "Little girl, you're happy with Me cleaning up your mess and with this little bit of life. Honey, you ain't seen nothing yet."

"That's great," I thought. But would you look at this clean yard with little flowers growing in it? It just can't get any better than this! Thank you, Jesus!"

And then in the final part of the dream, I was already in the old house. I came out on the front porch and couldn't believe my eyes. There was about an acre, a perfect rectangle (in reality, the yard is much smaller) that I knew was mine. Filling the borders was the most luscious, green, jungle-like scene—yet in perfect order. There were paths all through it. It was wild, but it wasn't chaotic at all. And in the center was a gazebo. The center, the gazebo, was calling for me. I thought I would lose my mind at the wonder of it all. I walked down the steps of my front porch and began to walk through this wild, green, wonderful place. And with every step I took, the green things would bloom as I walked by. And the colors! These weren't colors that you find in a Crayola box. These were colors I had never seen before. There are no words to de- scribe how I felt. When I woke, I knew that this dream was significant and that it was from the Lord.

Let me back up a bit to what preceded this dream. It was New Year's Eve 2009. I was ministering at a prison, and at the end of the service, an inmate who was in for life for murder approached me in tears. He handed me a torn yellow piece of paper and said this, "As you were speaking, the Lord told me to give this to you." On the paper was written, "Ezekiel 36: 33-36." Here's what it says:

"*Message of God, the Master:*

'On the day I scrub you clean from all your filthy living, I'll also make your cities livable. The ruins will be rebuilt. The neglected land will be worked again, no longer overgrown with weeds and thistles, worthless in the eyes of passersby. People will exclaim, "Why, this weed patch has been turned into a Garden of Eden! And the ruined cities, smashed into oblivion, are now thriving!" The nations around you that are still in existence will realize that I, God, rebuild ruins and replant empty waste places. I, God, said so, and I'll do it'

— The Message Bible(MSG).

At the time, I knew it meant something, and it humbled me to know that God would use any means to get a message to me. Even a prisoner.

The church I attended at the time always participated in a forty-day season of fasting and prayer. I looked forward to it every year. In previous years, the Lord had always given me a theme for those seasons. Sometimes it was a word; other times it was a Scripture. I knew for 2010 it would be Ezekiel 36:33-36.

I spent every day studying this text. I researched it word for word, up and down, inside and out. Honestly, I don't think I read anything else in the Word unless it paralleled or connected to Ezekiel 36. (I highly recommend this, by the way. This highly-focused season ended up being one of the richest studies I've ever done.)

On night thirty-seven of the forty days of fasting and prayer was the THE NIGHT. That was the night that God gave me **"The Dream."** I can count on one hand and still have fingers left over how many times that I know that I know that the Lord has spoken to me in a dream. I didn't understand what it all meant or the impact it would have or what period of time it was foretelling, but what I did know was that God had sent it to me. I didn't know if He was just showing me what heaven would look like. Or perhaps He was just giving me comfort for my present situation that certainly mirrored in the natural what the first part of the dream portrayed.

The dream impacted me so much that I felt I needed a witness to it. I wrote it on paper and gave it to my pastor's wife. After reading it, she agreed with me that it had to be from the Lord. She said, "Christy, I don't think this dream is just for you." Even now, when I think back on it, it's astounding that God would us a prisoner to speak to another "prisoner" (because that's what I was). But what He had done for me personally! Just a few verses back in that same chapter it says this:

> *"For here's what I'm going to do: I'm going to take you out of these countries, gather you from all over, and bring you back to your own land. I'll pour pure water over you and scrub you clean. I'll give you a new heart, put a new spirit in you. I'll remove the stone heart from your body and replace it with a heart that's God-willed,*

not self-willed. I'll put my Spirit in you and make it possible for you to do what I tell you and live by my commands."

— Ezekiel 36: 24-28(MSG)

Just like the dream, my life was a mess. There's too much to tell in this book! But He took years, and He began to purify me. He chiseled. He pruned. He cut. He burned. He literally removed my beaten-up and hardened heart and gave me a new one. He gave me a hope and a vision and a purpose. I had to die—so that I could live. I had to die so that He could get me focused on the center again. I had to get my eyes fixed on Jesus so that I could run the race set before me.

I'm a teacher and a speaker. I love to teach God's Word and God's love. A particular series that I was teaching in 2016 was supposed to conclude in six weeks but lasted for eleven months. The subject was the Holy Spirit. Women's hearts were so stirred. They didn't want it to end. From the overflow of that, a women's retreat was born. And from that retreat, more retreats were born. It was at that first retreat, on the last morning during worship, before I was to give the final message of the weekend, in what seemed like an hour but was really only about thirty seconds, God showed me that the entire next retreat would be based on the dream I'd had so many years ago.

A burden that God had placed on my heart and on my ministry team's hearts was for women of all ages, all backgrounds, all cultures, churched and un-churched to worship together, to serve together, to fellowship together—to walk alongside each other. In that moment, during worship, God asked me to turn around and look at all the women. What I saw were women of all ages, all backgrounds, all skin colors. It was one of the most beautiful sights I'd ever seen. And then as one of the younger women came up to play the flute and accompany the worship leader on the final worship song, God said to me, "See? I'm doing it. It's happening right now. And this is just the beginning." And He showed me the next retreat and how there would be a progression, just like in my dream. I knew in that moment that the blooms that opened as I walked by, the ones that were unique in colors never seen by the human eye, were THESE ladies and the ladies who would follow. I knew that He was telling me to bring them to **"The Garden."**

The theme scripture that God gave me for the Come to the Garden retreat was from Isaiah.

> *The Lord will guide you always; He will satisfy your needs in a sun-scorched land (barren, dead) And will strengthen your frame. You will be like a well-watered garden, Like a spring whose waters never fail.*
>
> — Isaiah 58:11, New International Version (NIV)

And that is exactly what happened. Sprinkled throughout this book are testimonies of what our God did for His daughters. I believe He will do the same for you, my friend. Which brings us here. "Come to the Garden" with us.

Chapter 1

It's Time for a Breakup

"Getting over a painful experience is much like crossing monkey bars. You have to let go at some point in order to move forward."

— C.S. Lewis

This is what the Sovereign Lord says: 'On the day I cleanse you from all your sins, I will resettle your towns, and the ruins will be rebuilt. The desolate land will be cultivated instead of lying desolate in the sight of all who pass through it. They will say, "This land that was laid waste has become like the garden of Eden; the cities that were lying in ruins, desolate and destroyed, are now fortified and inhabited." Then the nations around you that remain will know that I the Lord have rebuilt what was destroyed and have replanted what was desolate. I the Lord have spoken, and I will do it.'

— Ezekiel 36:33-36 (NIV)

Message of God, the Master: 'On the day I scrub you clean from all your filthy living, I'll also make your cities livable. The ruins will be rebuilt. The neglected land will be worked again, no longer overgrown with weeds and thistles, worthless in the eyes of passersby. People will exclaim, "Why, this weed patch has been turned into a Garden of Eden! And the ruined cities, smashed into oblivion, are now thriving!" The nations around you that are still in existence will realize that I, God, rebuild and replant empty waste places. I, God, said so, and I'll do it.'

— Ezekiel 36:33-36 (MSG)

I had a dream. The year was 2010, and I was on day thirty-seven of a forty-day fast that I had begun in January. I dreamt I pulled into the driveway of my place of business. (In reality, I owned a historic Victorian house that housed my business.) On with the dream. I pulled into the driveway and felt disgust and despair. I got out of the car and really wanted to get back in, drive away, and never come back. The yard was a mess. There was nothing growing, nothing green. Everything was dead. (In real life, I was continuously frustrated because I could never get grass to grow there because there was a giant magnolia tree in the center of the yard that shed leaves terribly.)

There were sticks and limbs and rotted leaves and stones, debris and dead things everywhere. I reached down to pick up a stick and thought to myself, "What's the point? There are thousands more." I felt so overwhelmed. I went in the old house so I wouldn't have to look at it anymore. When I came back out, I was stunned! I was overjoyed! I felt like I had a new lease on life! Although the ground was still brown, although there was nothing green, although there was nothing growing, all the debris, all the dead things had been removed. There was no life, but there was order. I cried out to God in delight, "Thank you, thank you, thank you!" I was so relieved. And

God spoke to me (not sure how to explain how He spoke, because it wasn't really an audible voice), "Christy (I imagined Him shaking His head in slight irritation), you are excited because I cleaned up your mess. You have no idea the plans I have for you, and they go way beyond Me just cleaning up your mess." I heard Him, but all I could take in at that moment was that He had removed all that was keeping me down. My burden had been lifted.

At this time in my life, I owned a business and the property that business was housed in, which was a gorgeous, white Victorian home with a wraparound porch that had been built in 1907. In the front yard was a massive magnolia tree. Even though it was beautiful, the leaves were a mess. No grass or anything else would grow, despite the efforts of multiple landscapers.

At the time of the dream, I was still feeling the results of the financial recession of 2008. I had many bills, and the property needed a great deal of repair because of things like roof and tree limb damage from storms. On top of this, I was financially struggling to make payroll. I had also been estranged from my son for a season, and even though tiny bits of progress had been made, there wasn't a day that my heart wasn't bleeding because of the distance between us.

This was also when we discovered the severity of my parents' situation. My nephew, a drug addict, had been stealing checks and property from them to support his addiction. They refused to press charges or hold him accountable. Our relationship became very strained, and I lived in a state of constant stomach churning.

On top of all this, I still couldn't get a blessed thing to grow on my property. Literally everything—physically, emotionally, and spiritually—seemed dead, including my dreams for my future. And so, on the night of the thirty-seventh day of my fast, after meditating day and night on the scriptures listed above, which had been given to me by a man who was in prison for life, I received the dream.

In the same way, on this first night of the Come to the Garden retreat, our decorations were barren and brown. There were sticks and debris around the altars and on the stage. I hope that you will open your imagination to our journey to the garden.

Chapter 2

Dead Things

"The trees are about to show you just how beautiful letting go can be."

— Anonymous

Have you ever had a tree pruned? Sometimes I've seen a landscaper cut the branches back so far it looks like there's nothing left. A tree can look totally destroyed, but the landscaper will always reply, "You just watch and see." Sure enough, before long, the tree is growing better and looking better than ever before.

Just like trees need pruning from time to time to remove dead branches or areas where there is overgrowth, you and I need to be pruned or reshaped at different times in different areas of our lives. It is never a pleasant experience; having things cut off is no fun and can be quite painful. But, like a tree, when the pruning is over, we're much better off and can grow like never before. God wants us at our very best—spiritually, emotionally, and physically.

Any branch in Me that does not bear fruit [that stops bearing] He cuts away [trims off, takes away]; and He cleanses and repeatedly prunes every branch that continues to bear fruit, to make it bear more and richer and more excellent fruit.

— John 15:2
Amplified Bible, Classic Edition(AMPC)

Some of us may be dragging around dead branches today. At the particular season in my life I've just described, I sure was. I had lost my peace; I had lost my joy; I had lost my trust. I was mad at God. Everything in the world was crumbling around me. I was still smarting over the fact that my ex-husband had poisoned the mind of my son, who was my heart. I was so bitter. I was trying to handle everything myself, trying to hustle money so I could pay my bills and take care of my payroll.

What dead branches are you dragging around? Maybe it's a bad relationship. Maybe it's guilt and shame. Maybe it's an old wound from your past. Maybe it's a negative attitude. It would be great if we had God's perspective all the time and could agree with Him and say, "Yes, God, let's get rid of that dead branch." Many times, however, we're too afraid to give up what we know for something new that we just can't see or understand.

The truth is, you can be miserable and dragging those dead things around forever, or you can go through the pain of letting God prune them away. God doesn't want to see us struggle. He loves us, and He will never give up on us.

Consider more about dead things. God cleans up the mess, and it's just the beginning. Disorder, chaos, anxiety, worry—there can be a removal of those things, even though the situation may look the same.

In my dream, the sticks and the dead things had been removed, but the ground was still barren, brown, and hard as a rock. In reality, I began to sense that a change was coming, but it wasn't to be in my circumstances yet. It was going to be in me. I was still in debt. There were relationships yet to be reconciled. But the ground of my heart had grown stone hard, and The Gardener can't work with hard ground. So He began to break up the hard and barren places of my heart.

> *Sow for yourselves righteousness; Reap in mercy; Break up your fallow ground, For it is time to seek the Lord, Till He comes and rains righteousness on you.*
>
> — Hosea 10:12 New King James Version (NKJV)

Breakups are hard. If you are looking for a breakthrough in your life or situation, there are first some things that need to break up concerning you personally. The fallow ground. Definition of fallow: Unplowed, not in use, unseeded. You will need to have a breakup with some things—some thought processes, some relationships, some addictions, some sin, some bondages, some lies, and some attitudes.

> *I will surely assemble all of you, O Jacob, I will surely gather the remnant of Israel; I will put them together like sheep of the fold, like a flock in the midst of their pasture; they shall make a loud noise because of so many people." (It's gone from an individual breakup.) "The one who breaks open will come up before them; they (plural) will break out, pass through the gate, and go out by it; their king will pass before them, with the Lord at their head.*
>
> — Micah 2:12-13 (NKJV)

God says you're going to have an individual breakup with some things in the fallow hardness of your heart. He says, "As you seek me, I'm going to break some of that up in you. But then I'm going to assign you to a gathering, to an assembling of people, and as you individually bring your breakups together, I will cause a spirit of breakout in that assembly of people."

As Verse 13 says, *"They will break out."* And when they break out, the gate will open, and the King will come in! Welcome to the breakup that will lead to the breakout which is going to be your breakthrough!

Your enemy has tried to hold you in, to make you think you'll never get rid of the dead things in your life, that there will always be chaos and mess, that nothing can ever live on that barren ground.

But if one can put a thousand to flight, and two can put ten thousand to flight, imagine how much breakout power we have as believers united together reading this book! Break up. Break out.

Once you have a breakup personally, on the inside, with lukewarmness, relationships that have hindered you, laziness, and whatever else has held you down, then you come together in a breakout assembly.

I know that as you read, there are going to be some breakups in your heart and some breakouts among those who take these teachings to heart. Miracles, a new anointing, a new calling, a new attitude, a new direction, a deeper place with God. The rain will fall in the Spirit, and the King is going to come through the gate.

And David said with longing, "Oh, that someone would give me a drink of the water from the well of Bethlehem, which is by the gate!" So the three mighty men broke through the camp of the Philistines, drew water from the well of Bethlehem that was by the gate, and took it and brought it to David.

— 2 Samuel 23:15-16 (NKJV)

If you have a breakup with some things and then come where two or three are gathered, an assembly, then they will have a breakout of limitations. And God will bring you a breakthrough.

Notice that the breakthrough has to do with the enemy's front lines. The Philistines controlled the territory where fresh water was. These mighty men said, "Our king wants some fresh water," and because there had already been a breakup and a breakout, they were going to have a breakthrough. Right through the enemy's lines.

There is a pattern and a formula for breakthrough. All dead things have to be removed. It starts with brokenness. Break up the fallow ground. Ground that was once fruitful. Ground that once produced the fruit of the Spirit: love, joy, peace, long suffering, kindness, goodness, faithfulness, gentleness, and self-control. The areas that are no longer fruitful have to be broken up.

God needs the ground to be broken up so that the seed of His Word will fall and begin to produce the fruit of the Spirit once again, as well as forgiveness and healing. Brokenness on earth brings openness in heaven. If you break up the hard ground, God said the rain will fall. The rain in heaven is attracted to the brokenness on earth, but there has to be a breaking up that happens inside of us through repentance, through surrender, through fasting, through prayer, and through praise.

We have to break up the fallow ground, and then the whole assembly gathers together. That's what happened during my forty days of fasting and prayer. That's what we are talking about right now.

When my home church live streams worship services, thousands are watching, and we've had folks who are suicidal have a change of heart. We've had supernatural healings because of the sacred assembly. Leading up to that kind of service, there is always a breaking up of things. It always leads to a breaking out and then inevitably to a breakthrough.

The same thing is set up for you now. The breaking up began a long time ago. You have been covered in prayer for months. My ministry team, our prayer warriors, and myself have prayed for each and every one of you! The Lord will complete what He has started.

Breakthrough can happen in the life of every person reading this book.

What exactly does "break out" mean? The Scripture says, "The gate will open, and the King will come through." What are we going to break out of as a sacred assembly? How about breaking out of self-imposed limitations?

- Break out of our inferiority.
- Break out of our imprisoning pasts.
- Break out of the baggage.
- Break out of the depression.
- Break out of the cycles of addiction.
- Break out of the poverty mindsets.
- Break out of the self-defeating mentality.
- Break out of people's opinion of you. (That's one of the best ones—I can testify to that!)
- Break out of the "It's never been done this way before" mentality.

When a person has a breakup, God puts us together, and a spirit of breakthrough comes on that sacred assembly. We begin to break out of the mentality that says, "It's never been done." We have to break out before we can have a breakthrough. A breakout has to do with your mind, your mentality.

You begin to believe God CAN. You break up with all those things that have held you. Then you break out, like a small shoot of a plant. The lines of limitation are broken, and then you have a breakthrough to fresh water. The breakthrough of the enemy's lines is where we're headed.

Pat O'Brien won a gold medal in the Olympics in the 1940s. He threw the shot put, which is a heavy metal ball. You run to a line, stop, and throw. Pat O'Brien could throw it sixteen feet, and he set a world record. Even though he already had the record, one year he decided to try throwing the shot put a different way. He decided to twirl instead of just running straight like everyone had always done.

The iron ball was the same, but he decided to try a new method with a new passion, and by twirling, he threw it seventeen feet. He broke his own world record. He broke out of the self-imposed rules that stopped him. I'm not satisfied with what I, or this ministry, did last year. You shouldn't be satisfied with what you did, either. We need to break out of those self imposed limitations.

Some people, churches, and organizations are memory-driven instead of vision-driven. We get accustomed to how it used to be done and has always been done, but I believe God is calling us to greater things.

Once, a man did a scientific experiment where he took fleas and put them into a jar. Later on, even when he took the lid off, the fleas would only jump as high as they had gotten used to jumping in the jar. They didn't realize things had changed. Their limitations were dictated by their past experiences that said, "You can't ever go any higher than this, so just give up." They even passed that mentality on to their offspring.

Some of you have a flea mentality. You've convinced yourselves that because you tried and failed in the past, you can't go any higher. But the God of your breakup, your breakout, and your breakthrough is with you right now. And the lid has been removed! It's time to break through to a new level and dimension of victory and faith in God. You are either a "God CAN" or a "God CAN'T" person. Today may be just the beginning of the removal of dead things, chaos, and barrenness. Don't let your present trouble name your future.

In the Bible, the glorious Ark of the Covenant was stolen by the Philistines. On that same day, a mother named her baby the worst name imaginable—Ichabod, which means, "The Glory has Departed." In other words, she was naming her future by her present and past circumstances.

As you read this, your ground may seem barren and littered with dead branches, but never name your future by the trouble of your past or present circumstances. Your future will be fruitful and full of life. The desolate places will become like the Garden of Eden. God is taking you where you've never been before. That baby should have been named Immanuel—"God is with Me."

The enemy has a lid on some jars today. Because you've gone

through a divorce, an abortion, a bankruptcy, or the loss of a child or other loved one, the enemy has told you, "Just stay where you are." But God has brought you here to have a breakup, so you can have a breakout, so that you'll leave here with a breakthrough.

The breakthrough has to do with the enemy's front line. He expects you to run away, but we are running toward. We are going to break through the enemy lines. The Gates of Hell will not prevail against the daughters and sons of God.

There's a country song that says: You get your house back, your dog back, your truck back, your hair back. We're running to the enemy's lines, not away, and we're going to get our families back, our dreams back, our children back, and our marriages back.

Don't ever speak words of death over your life. Don't ever let the Devil think he's winning. He's already lost. My family is saved. My children are saved. My family is blessed. My family is anointed. My family is consecrated, sanctified and holy unto God.

That's what we say as we break through the enemy's front lines. Break up. That's me. Break out. That's us. That's what we're feeling right now. And then break through the enemy's front line.

Don't play the Devil's advocate, asking, "What if it doesn't happen? What if I don't get a job? What if my marriage ends in divorce? What if my kids don't come back? What if I lose my house?" No.

What if God does? Won't He do it? You can build that business back up. You can go to college. You can get your finances in order. You can get restoration in your marriage. Your kids are God's kids, and He will take care of them. You can buy that house. You can be free from addictions. You can see your family saved.

The Bible says that *"He that is in you is greater."* The Bible also says, in 2 Kings 6:16 (NKJV), *"Do not fear, for those who are with us are more than those who are with them."* Why should the "more" honor the "less?" The Devil is less, so why should the more in us honor the less in him?

It's time for a breakup. Breakups are rarely easy, but that's why we're here—for a breakup, a breakout, and a breakthrough.

Jesus had to break up the fallow ground in the Garden of

Gethsemane. He had to say, *"Not my will, but yours."* His sweat became drops of blood. There was a breakup of His will. Then He had a breakout. They put Him in the tomb, but on the third day, He rolled the stone away. And He broke out.

The jaws of death couldn't hold Him, and now He comes for you and me and says, "You can have a breakthrough." Never go back where you came from—that addiction, that shame, that sin, that bondage, those lies, or those bad decisions. Breakthrough. He gives us that authority in His name. Sometimes God will break you in so He can break you out and give others a breakthrough by what you went through. Maybe you feel barren, desolate, like a desert. You feel so remote you're not even sure God can reach you or find you.

One of the theme verses for our ministry is Ezekiel 47:9 (NIV): *"Swarms of living creatures will live wherever the river flows. There will be large numbers of fish, because this water flows there and makes the salt water fresh; so where the river flows everything will live."*

> *Fishermen will stand along the shore; from En Gedi to En Eglaim there will be places for spreading nets.*
> — Ezekiel 47:10 (NIV)

There was a news story from a few years ago. *National Geographic* did a feature on it. A small village in Australia is about 500 miles inland. The population is 669 people. They are about 500 full miles from any body of water. One day, clouds blew in, and not only did rain fall from the sky, but so did fish.

Some of the fish were frozen, and some hit the ground flopping. There's no river or coastline nearby, so scientists believe that a tornado went over a body of water and sucked the fish up into the air. Meteorologists believe the fish could have been scooped up to 50,000 feet into the air. Once they get that high, they freeze, so a wind blew in and blew clouds 500 miles inland to an atmosphere that was warm enough to melt the fish, and they started falling out of the sky.

The fish were a type of perch, and so many rained down from the sky that it took the people in the village seven days to collect them all. When God gets ready to send your harvest, it doesn't matter where you're located. If He says it's your season and your time, He'll let it rain fish on your desolate and barren desert.

Fruit trees of all kinds will grow on both banks of the river. Their leaves will not wither, nor will their fruit fail. Every month they will bear fruit, because the water from the sanctuary flows to them. Their fruit will serve for food and their leaves for healing.

— Ezekiel 47:12 (NIV)

We read in Ezekiel that God said, "On that day that I cleanse you the ruins will be rebuilt." What are the dead things in your life that need to be removed? In my dream, I was relieved just to have the mess cleaned up. The ground was still brown, but all the dead things were gone. It was where He wanted me to start.

God goes on to say in Ezekiel, "The desolate land will be cultivated instead of being a desolation in the sight of everyone who passes by." When the dead things are removed, it's time to break up the ground. What things are you holding onto that have hardened you?

Is there unforgiveness that you have been carrying around with you like a dead tree? Is it guilt and shame? Maybe it's mistakes in your past. Maybe it's lukewarmness in your spiritual walk. Maybe you've struggled with self-image issues your entire life. Today is the day to let God remove the dead things. Today is the day God wants to break up your fallow ground.

Chapter 3

Vanessa

Vanessa Reflecting on the time at the Come to the Garden Retreat, a part of me was scared. I didn't know what going to happen there. For a few months leading up to the retreat, God had spoken to me about how He was going to expand me, and I just needed to trust in Him more, even though I already did. He was faithful to what He had spoken to me leading up to that weekend. The night before the retreat, He was talking to me, telling me to meet Him and to be vulnerable and transparent toward what was to come. He said to be transparent to those I was going to meet and talk to and just to be vulnerable and open to the Holy Spirit. Little did I realize that I was going on a journey—an incredible journey was waiting for me there.

After I arrived in Lake Placid and went to see where I was staying and who my roommates were, I was at ease. I decided on a bed across from a wonderful friend, Ashleydawn, someone I hadn't seen in a while as a result of my work schedule, church, and life in general. It was just nice to see her. Having the Florida School of Discipleship girls in the bunk area was just entertaining, to say the least. I've never met a group of girls who were so on fire for Christ and spoke with such conviction; it was incredible.

The first night of service was incredible, and I could sense the Holy Spirit there in that building. I knew something was going to happen. The next morning, I was having my quiet time, and a sense of peace came over me as soon as I opened my Bible. The first thing

I opened to was Isaiah 38, which talks about Hezekiah's illness and that he had a message for Isaiah. As I read, it spoke to me, especially verses 19 and 20: "The living, the living—they praise you, as I am doing today; fathers tell their children about your faithfulness. The Lord will save me, and we will sing with stringed instruments all the days of our lives in the temple of the Lord." As the sunrise was happening, I was getting ready for what was to come.

As I prepared for evening service, I took the time during the day to focus on me. I walked around the property and even was able to get a nap in, taking advantage of the time.

When I finally walked into the service, I was given a seed. It represented the things that I needed to plant, what needed to be either let go of or needed to grow. As Christy spoke, the Lord spoke to me in the way only He could. He spoke a truth to my heart, and as I listened to Him and to the message, the Prayer of Jabez came to mind. I remembered something God had spoken to me about expanding me and that I needed to let go—let go of the pain and sorrow of my grandmother's death that had hit me so hard. Let go of the hurt and damage that people had caused me. I needed to just release it to my Father and let Him handle it. The part of the prayer that spoke to me most was when Jabez cried out to the God of Israel, "Oh, that you bless me and enlarge my territory." That's when I knew what I needed to do: Take a leap of faith and let Him do what He needed to do. At the altar call, I went boldly and faithfully up to Pastor Phyllis and told her that I was ready to expand myself and take a leap. She knew my story and knew how hard it was for me to say that out loud. She asked me if I had been baptized in the Holy Spirit. I replied, "No."

She said, "I think it's time." It was then that a full surrendering took place. As I was open to what the Holy Spirit did, there was a fire that took place inside of me.

After receiving the Holy Spirit, I realized that on this very day eight years prior, I had been baptized by immersion. If you study numbers in the Bible, you know the meaning of numbers can be very important. Seven indicates a completion, but the number eight often symbolizes new life and new beginnings. Not only I was beginning something new, but He created me newly. During the Saturday morning session, God proved Himself even more. My gift from the raffle that morning was a Bible titled the Beyond Suffering Bible, which is fitting for what my life up to that point had been. I had suffered loss, abandonment, abuse, depression, anxiety, the death of those close to me, and more. Receiving this Bible was God's gift for me. Knowing that I needed it, He reminded me of the lavishness of His capability on my behalf. That afternoon, during down time, I decided to open it, and it opened to Hannah's Prayer in the book of 1 Samuel 2:1-10. Even though it was about bearing a baby, it still spoke to me and revealed to me more of what God needed to show me.

Walking into Saturday evening service was like dream filled with flowers, trees, and foliage. It was just beautiful. Stepping into the room was like entering Christy's dream she'd had a few years prior. Instead of the seeds we'd planted the night before, there were now papier mache flowers, and under each was a word and a verse associated with that word. The key was picking a flower, and that flower was meant to be yours. I went up, picked my flower, and the phrase I got was, "New Spirit," with the verse Ezekiel 36:26: "I will give you a new heart and put a new spirit in you; I will remove from you your heart of stone and give you a heart of flesh." This was a verse that I've been praying over people in my life without realizing I needed it more. It showed God's grace and blessing over my life and my daughters' lives.

As the weekend was coming to an end, I spent the morning just soaking in what had happened and anticipating God's plans. I spent my morning devotion by the water to let Him reveal Himself during my quiet time with Him. Going into the last session of the weekend was the cherry on top for me. There was a stirring in me that was needing releasing and a word that needed to be heard. I remember being in awe and wanting to boldly speak a word that I've seen so many times in my life. It was during worship that I heard Him say, "Open and speak." it was then a word came out of me, a moment that my faith was stretched further. Knowing that our Father, our Lord, knows the deepest desire of our hearts was a comforting thought for me. After I spoke the word, there was a burning, like my heart was on fire inside of me. He was removing my heart of stone and placing a new heart and spirit in me. I wasn't going to be the same after that.

During the final altar call, He called me by name. It was there that I had some unfinished business. I had received two visions. One was of a garden and Jesus waiting for me. As I entered the garden, I met Him. He was speaking to me, showing me things that were hidden deep down inside me. I had some deep roots I didn't know were there, causing me pain. I had stuffed my grief and guilt from my grandmother's death inside; I had forgotten it was there. He needed me to let it go. It was then that He took the all the pain inside away. He started to clip the dead branches that needed to go. He watered me, so the roots that needed watering could grow. He then spoke to me about my girls and how they were protected, that He was holding them close to Him. And that I needed to forgive myself.

The next vision was of a book. It opened to my name. Under my name were names, lies, and everything else the enemy had told me, written out. God took His hand and wiped everything clean. But then He wrote all the names and truths I am to Him. It was there I left a life I had once known and started a new life. When I got up from the floor, I had a new sense of everything. I knew that I was about to leave the garden and go back my community and be the person I had started to become there in the garden. My time there was brief, but it was worth it. I have never been the same since that weekend. My coworkers saw something different the next day, and I just smiled and said that you had to be there to understand. God continues to bless me and remains faithful to everything He told me—that I go down but upward. And He deserves all the glory for it.

Chapter 4

Miggie

Oh, the things the Lord was already doing among our ladies before this retreat! We were all excited and anticipating what He was going to do in those who would be attending Come to the Garden. In expectation, our team prayed and fasted for the lives of each woman who would enter the gates.

We planned, we organized, and we fasted, but, most of all, we prayed. We knew God was going to show up in a big way. The River Dwellers ministry had begun, and the testimonies of the lives being touched were unbelievable. But oh, the anticipation of what was going to come for our ladies! I was never expecting, yet I was hopefully wishing for what God would do in my life. To begin with, the weeks of fasting before the retreat were miraculous.

You see, I was a grandchild of two Pentecostal ministers and the daughter of a Minister of Music. I was raised in the church, sleeping on the pews and attending church four to five times a week. At an early age, I accepted the Lord, and God used my life in wonderful ways. When I was a young teenager, the Lord would give me visions and give me words of prophesy and encouragement for individuals and the church. I loved the Lord so much. Then, life happened, and I strayed from the Lord as a young adult, because, you know, sometimes we think we know it all and we can do it on our own. I know that the Lord never left me; I just put Him in the closet, because that was just convenient for me at that time of my life, or so I thought. But God had other plans.

Fast forward years later, and I was once again serving the Lord, but never feeling worthy. I prayed diligently to feel that closeness to my Father up in heaven. I wanted to feel Him closer than my skin, to hear His sweet whispers in my ear. I had grieved the Holy Spirit, and I knew it, but in praying for all of our ladies, God began to open my ears, my heart, and my life once again to all that He wanted me to feel.

October came, and we were inviting ladies into the sanctuary of the Lord. All were excited, and the worship was deeply blessed. The Lord was moving, and to see women's faces and lives changing before our eyes was a precious gift for all of us. This is what we had prayed for; this is what the Lord wanted to give all of us. As I was praying on the prayer team, the Lord opened my heart, my eyes, and my ears. I saw angels before me once again; I could see them praising along-side of us, and I could feel the joy in God's heart as the worship rose up as a sweet fragrance. I could feel His presence on my skin, and I allowed myself to open up and let the Holy Spirit speak a word of edification to the ladies through me. You see, it is not that God had removed Himself from me, but that I had allowed the enemy to make me think that I was not worthy for God to love me or use me. He had been there all along, waiting for me to allow Him back in. Trust in your Father God. He is with you always; do not let the enemy steal your joy and all that He has for you. He is just waiting for you to ask and receive. He stands with open arms waiting for you to enter in.

Chapter 5

Roots

All things must come to the soul from its roots, from where it is planted.

—Saint Teresa of Avila

Before they call I will answer: while they are still speaking I will hear.

— Isaiah 65:24 (NIV)

This is God saying, "I am so passionate about blessing you that I just can't wait for you to call on Me. I'm going to bless you before you call because I know what you need before you know what you need. And when you finally get to the place where you speak to Me, I'm already hearing you." This is the great passion of God on our behalf. Please don't skim over this. Isaiah is talking about a day, our day, that before you call "I will answer, and while you're praying about it, I've already taken care of it."

For you meet him with the blessings of goodness; you set a crown of pure gold upon his head.

— Psalm 21:3 (NKJV)

What David is saying in this particular Psalm is that when I feel defeated, *"You present me with blessings of goodness."* God is already there with outstretched hands, full of blessings. It goes on to say, *"You set a crown of pure gold upon his head."*

Let me tell you why David wrote that Psalm: It was the result of a battle that Israel went through. David found out the Assyrians had hired other enemies of Israel to join them and go against him. David and his forces were outnumbered in every way possible. He cried out to the Lord, and the Lord soundly defeated the Assyrians and the Ammonites. SOUNDLY defeated them. It was an embarrassing defeat for them, and that's when David wrote that Psalm. He was on a high. He was elated. He was on a mountain. He said, "Look, victory is ours!"

In another reference to that battle, he said, "God has put them under our feet." But what David didn't realize was that he hadn't killed the enemy. He had just driven them back. And while David was rejoicing and writing and singing and dancing about his victory over the enemy, the enemy was strengthening itself and planning another attack.

The enemy always comes back. He can be held back, and he can be paralyzed through your prayers, but as long as you are living, there will always be another greater and stronger attack. The Devil is furious that we have authority over him, and until Jesus comes back, he will always try to convince us that we don't.

We get very elated when we have a victory, but hear me right now: Don't ever take your armor off! For me, it seems like the higher I go spiritually, the lower my next valley seems to be. I can be on the mountain and tend to forget that a valley usually comes after a mountain, and the valley seems to go way lower than the one before, but it catches me off guard most times. However, the mountaintop experiences tend to be higher also. It's continually higher and lower events and higher and lower emotions in my life.

Don't forget that! If you do, you'll start blaming yourself that you let the enemy come back. You'll start feeling guilty. "Well, is there some sin in my life I still haven't asked forgiveness for?" And then you start focusing on yourself and your weakness, rather than understanding that this is life.

This is the battle that Scripture talks about over and over. This is the Christian walk. This is the Christian warfare. I often wonder why God does things the way He does them. It doesn't make any sense to my human brain.

I think about Moses. Why didn't God just take him out to the wilderness with the people? Why did God allow him to murder someone first? What was the point of that? He could have raised David up to kingship without David committing adultery. Why allow him to murder? Why would God allow him to live in a lie for so long? Why would God allow everything inside of David to be destroyed and then use David's own sin? Why would God let Peter do worse than Moses or David? Peter denied Jesus, but then just a few days later, Peter was filled with the Holy Spirit and stood up and preached the Gospel of Jesus.

Why does God allow someone to murder? Why does God allow someone to cheat? Why does God allow someone to deny Him boldly and then use them? I just can't figure God out.

I want to know why I have to go down before He can raise me up. What is it about my weakness that glorifies God? What is it about my inability to be consistent? What is it about my unfaithfulness that somehow brings God into play in my life?

Maybe you'd be surprised to know that every time I bring the Gospel, I feel less qualified than the last time. I feel less capable than I did the day before. All I know is that God chooses people whom we wouldn't choose. When He chooses you, He never un-chooses you. Once God possesses you, you are His for eternity. God always makes up for those days on the playground when you were the last one picked.

You've been bought with a price, and that price was the blood of Jesus. You belong to Him. So, whatever He decides to do and use in your life is God's business. Some of you tonight are trying to figure out why you still wrestle with some weaknesses. Some of you thought you had victory over it, but it comes back. Why?

Let's talk about a story I'll call *"Fancy Night at Belle Vive."* The name of my previous business, a day spa, was Belle Vive, which means "beautiful living." Not long after opening, we had an invitation-only open house. We went all out. From the beautiful invitations, to the strung lights outside, to the gurgling fountain. The building (the same building from my dream) was a 120-year-old Victorian house with a very large front porch, a porch swing, and spacious sitting areas. On this night, the porch and the outside were full of men and women in formal evening wear, champagne glasses in hand. When you walked into the house, you would find a violinist playing, elegant hors d'oeuvres. It was truly a beautiful evening. The atmosphere was very festive; our town hadn't had a business like this before. I had completely remodeled the entire house. It was stunning. Original chandeliers, beautiful murals on the walls. It truly stood up to it's name, "belle." All of my employees were present for our grand opening event. Included in the mix were about six girls who were spa techs. Their job for the evening was to give guests tours of the treatment rooms at the spa.

As I was coming down the grand staircase after giving a tour to close friends of mine, I saw one of the spa techs at the bottom of the stairs looking at me with a helpless expression. She took me aside and said, "We have a slight problem." She took me into one the bathrooms, which was beautiful, by the way. It had a Jacuzzi tub that we used for treatments, there was an original chandelier in there, a beautiful mural on the wall, and a vast selection of spa salts and scrubs to sample. But, in the midst of the beauty, there, before my eyes, the Jacuzzi had turned into a brown fountain! There literally was brown water popping up from the drain. If I'd had time to enjoy the moment rather than panic, I would have admired how pretty the "fountain" was. And then more reports were coming in that all the toilets and all the sinks and all the showers and all the tubs now had "fountains" of brown water bubbling up out of them. We had a problem. Thankfully, until the evening was over, we were able to cover up our dilemma. But, as soon as the party was over, I was on the phone. A plumber came at 11:00 p.m. Then a special team came in and worked all night long. They had to dig down ten feet. There had been a tree there that had been cut down, but the ROOT had remained.

Let me reiterate: The plumber had to call a special team. They had to go down ten feet. Now, understand. The tree had been cut down. The tree was gone. But the root—remained. Believe it or not, there was enough moisture that the roots continued to expand, trying to keep the stump alive.

We had made it beautiful. Oh, it was so beautiful. We had covered it up. We had painted. We had wallpapered. But then it started to come up—from an unknown, underground source—and did I ever pay the price. It cost me, not just lots of money, but loss of productivity and aggravation. I was still finding roots after that.

While I had the property, we went through this same process two more times. What's the point? There's a reason there's one battle after another. You get one thing fixed, and you think, "This is done." You've cleaned it up. You paint it. You put makeup on it. You buy new clothes. "I'm fixed," you declare. The tree has been cut down. You've been forgiven and washed clean by the blood of Jesus.

But there's still some rootage. There's still some rootage in you, and there's still some rootage in me. In everyone. There's some rootage underground, way down deep in the dark. That can prevent the flow from being able to freely disperse itself. It can clog up everything, and about the time you think you can flush, you know the rest.

As long as you're alive, you're going to have to deal with rootage. With backup. Clogs. Lack of drainage. Smelly stuff. Ugly stuff. Dark and muddy stuff. You can act like everything is all right. You can come to church and raise your hands and shout. Then, by Tuesday, the woman who gets on your last nerve at work has done it again. You feel anger begin to rise up again. You'd been getting along well with your husband, but then things seem off again. Bitterness starts to rise to the top again. Maybe it's prejudice. Maybe lust, greed, strife, addiction, anger, resentment, hate, envy, or jealousy. These things can begin to seep through the old roots again.

Pursue peace with all people, and holiness, without which no one will see the Lord: looking carefully lest anyone fall short of the grace of God; lest any root of bitterness spring up causing trouble, and by this many become defiled;

— Hebrews 12:14-15 (NKJV)

Many become defiled. Entire families are destroyed because of a root of bitterness. Bitter roots deceive. The root of all roots is bitterness. There's always a little bit of truth in a root of bitterness.

Paul said, "But I fear, lest somehow, as the serpent deceived Eve by his craftiness, so your minds may be corrupted from the simplicity that is in Christ" (2 Corinthians 11:3, NKJV). Bitter roots defile. This is defined in Greek as "stain." It actually means "to dye."

Someone says, "How can I ever have joy or freedom with my past?" Every time she looks back, all she sees are the stains. That's another deception. You see, all the stains are covered by the blood of Jesus. They've been removed, as the Bible says, "Your sins were as crimson and are now as white as snow."

Roots of bitterness can be toward other people, but sometimes they're toward God. "God, you could have done something." We see this with Ruth's mother-in-law in the Old Testament.

But she said to them, 'Do not call me Naomi; call me Mara, the Almighty has dealt very bitterly with me.'

— Ruth 1:20 (NKJV)

Mara means bitter. Naomi is saying, "God did this to me." Our resentment, many times, isn't as much to do with a person as it is directed toward God. Why didn't God stop this? Why did God allow me to go through this? Maybe God didn't cause it, but He could have stopped it. Why didn't God stop the abuse? Why didn't He do something to the person who wronged me? And then how hard is it to see that same person who wronged you actually get blessed by God?

That raises the question, "How could God bless a person who does another person wrong?" The answer is, the same way He blesses you and me. We've all done somebody wrong. He blesses us because He's a merciful God.

The root of bitterness is a root that most of us, not just a few, need to have pulled out of our lives. God, why wasn't I loved better by my parents? Why did my marriage end? Why didn't you make me beautiful like her? Why didn't you give me talent like that? How could you let church people treat me like that? How could you let my loved one die? Why did my business fail? Why did I lose my job? I thought God was sovereign. He could have stopped it.

You see, that's not what sovereignty does. Yes, God is the supreme ruler of the universe, but He will never act outside of His character. In His sovereignty, He decided He didn't want robots, so He gave us a will. He created us in His image, but because we have a free will, we messed it all up in the beginning, and as a result of our actions, there is sin and sickness in the world. Things happen because we live in a fallen world, and we have a very real enemy. We have to be careful, because if we follow the line of thinking that God could or should have, we will have a root of bitterness toward God. We don't have to have bitter roots. Instead of bitter roots, how can we have better roots?

A man is not established by wickedness, But the root of the righteous cannot be moved.
— Proverbs 12:3 (NKJV)

The wicked covet the catch of evil men, But the root of the righteous yields fruit.
— Proverbs 12:12 (NKJV)

If you want to have better roots, better roots must be planted.

And the remnant who have escaped the house of Judah shall AGAIN take root downward and bear fruit upward.
— 2 Kings 19:30 (NKJV)

Shall AGAIN. Shall AGAIN take root downward and bear fruit upward. If you want to bear fruit, you have to take root. I love the word AGAIN here. In this Scripture, Judah had messed up. Judah shall AGAIN take root downward.

Have you ever messed up? The Word of the Lord tells us that if you've messed up, you can take root again. We all have areas in our lives that have good fruit, and we may have areas in our lives that have bad fruit. In the areas of our lives where we do not have good fruit, take root.

If you're having problems in your marriage, go to a marriage conference. Read a good Christian book about marriage. If you're having problems with your finances, take a Dave Ramsey class. Get into a small group that deals with the area you are struggling in. In other words, where you have bad fruit, take root AGAIN!

Maybe you've messed up, but don't get discouraged, take root AGAIN! Seeds have to be planted. Better roots must be grown. It's not enough to just spread seeds onto the surface of the ground once per week. You can't just have this seed of the Word spread on you once through this book. You're going to have to plant the seed.

Those who are planted in the house of the Lord Shall flourish in the courts of our God. They shall still bear fruit in old age; They shall be fresh and flourishing,
Psalm 92:13 (NKJV)

Who is going to bear fruit in old age? Who is going to be fresh and flourishing? Those who are planted in the house of the Lord. You need to get planted, at a local church, at a small group, at a place where you can flourish. It doesn't say those who just attend. It says those who are planted in the house of the Lord. Better roots must be planted, and they must be watered.

Blessed is the man who trusts in the Lord, and whose hope is the Lord. For he shall be like a tree planted by the waters, which spreads out its roots by the river, and will not fear when heat comes; (NO FEAR) but its leaf will be green, and will not be anxious in the year of drought, (NO ANXIETY) nor will cease from yielding fruit.
— Jeremiah 17:7-8 (NKJV)

He shall be like a tree planted by the rivers of water,
that brings forth its fruit in its season, whose leaf also
shall not wither; and whatever he does shall prosper.

— Psalm 1:3 (NKJV)

WHATEVER he does shall prosper. You get planted in the House of God, and you start meditating on the Word of God. WHATEVER you do will prosper. Reading the Word of God, meditating on the Word of God, studying the Word of God, praying the Word of God, and being planted in the House of God—this is watering the roots.

The Word of God is water in Scripture. Get into the Word of God in any area you need. For instance, if you're having financial problems, see what the Word of God says about it. If you're having marital problems, see what the Word of God says about it. Get into the Word of God about areas in your life where you have bad roots. By doing that, you'll start watering the good roots. Better roots must be watered. There's someone else who would like to water you as well. His name is Satan.

So the serpent spewed water out of his mouth like a flood
after the woman (church), that he might cause her to be
carried away by the flood.

— Revelation 12:15 (NKJV)

Have you ever had a flood of words come against you? When that happens, you need to raise up a standard against it. This is the only standard you can raise up against a flood of words from the enemy. Better roots must be planted, better roots must be watered, and better roots must be fertilized.

He also spoke this parable: 'A certain man had a fig tree planted in his vineyard, and he came seeking fruit on it and found none. Then he said to the keeper of his vineyard, "Look, for three years I have come seeking fruit on this fig tree and find none. Cut it down; why does it use up the ground?" But he answered and said to him, "Sir, let it alone this year also, until I dig around it (TREE) and fertilize it. And if it bears fruit, well. But if not, after that you can cut it down.'

— Luke 13:6-10 (NKJV)

If you have an area in your life that is not bearing good fruit, you need to fertilize it. What does that mean? Water means the Word of God. Well, fertilizer is manure. How many of you have some manure in your life? What is fertilizer? It's going through tough times and pressing into God. It's prayer.

Why? Because when we go through those tough times, we cry out to God. We call out to God. We spend time with God.

He saying, "Listen, this is an area that's not bearing fruit. Let's cut it down," and the guy says, "Wait, wait, wait! Let's dig around it. Let's get the weeds away from it. Let's clear the bad roots and the thorns. Let's get all the bad stuff out, and let's put some fertilizer on it."

Have you ever gotten out of your car only to be met with the fertilizer smell? It doesn't smell good, but it's going to make everything really pretty. Some of you have some circumstances in your life that smell like manure, but if you turn to the Lord, what's going to happen will blow you away.

Listen, when someone messes with you, they mess with God's kids. The enemy is messing with you. That means he's messing with one of God's kids. If you'll put your trust in God, if you'll rip out the bad roots, and if you'll put down some better roots, God will ALWAYS come to your defense. He will defend you.

We read the parable of the fig tree from Luke 13. I've always wondered about the meaning of the parable. He said, *"I've been looking for good fruit from this vineyard for three years now. Let's just rip it out. Cut it down."* And the vine keeper said, *"Lord, give me one more year. Give me one more year to try to water and fertilize these roots and see if we can get some good out of this tree."*

I need to say something pretty strongly. I feel like God has been waiting on some of you for a while. When I read that, I feel like I'm saying to the Lord, "Lord, the ones who aren't serving you or haven't been walking with you, Lord, the ones who aren't bearing fruit—give them a little more time."

I really believe that in the areas where you have bad fruit, you have to decide to do something about it, and you can. You can AGAIN take root downward and bear fruit upward. And the God of Israel will come to your defense.

> *Message of God, the Master: 'On the day I scrub you clean from all your filthy living, I'll also make your cities livable. The ruins will be rebuilt. The neglected land will be worked again, no longer overgrown with weeds and thistles, worthless in the eyes of passersby. People will exclaim, 'Why, this weed patch has been turned into a Garden of Eden! And the ruined cities, smashed into oblivion, are now thriving!' The nations around you that are still in existence will realize that I, God, rebuild ruins and replant empty waste places. I, God, said so, and I'll do it.'*
>
> — Ezekiel 33:33-36 (MSG)

That was New Year's Eve, 2010. I began a forty-day fast in January. This was my focus, and on day thirty-seven, I had my dream.

In the previous section we began the process of removing dead limbs from our lives, habits and behaviors that are holding us back. We began allowing the Lord to start breaking up the fallow ground in our hearts. Although breaking up is a painful part, it's a necessary step before planting. Now we've looked at our roots and the fertilizer we need to grow, all the mess, the past, the lessons, the tests, the learning, and adjusting. It takes time, but then it's time to plant the seeds.

Chapter 6

Edma

In the spring of 2017, my husband and I found out we were expecting. We were overjoyed. Our precious little boy or girl would complete our family. We were excited to see how our little angel would be woven into our tapestry. Fourteen weeks later, after receiving clearance from our doctor, we announced to our family and friends that we would be adding one more member to our family. Excitement and anticipation filled our home. A blueberry-sized little person in my womb was multiplying by 100 cells per minute, and morning sickness was in full swing.

Our excitement quickly turned into a horrific nightmare. One Saturday morning, I woke up drenched in blood. Everything came to a screeching halt. There was an immediate physical and mental debate. My eyes confirmed something was terribly wrong, but my mind refused to subscribe. Hopeful, I thought to myself perhaps I was hemorrhaging because of a perfectly treatable cause. I called my doctor right away, bracing myself for the inevitable command to hastily make my way to the emergency room. The joy and anticipation of seeing our baby was now accompanied by the heaviness of knowing we might lose her. I arrived at the hospital twenty minutes after speaking with my doctor. Shortly after a preliminary assessment, the physician came in, asked a few questions, and ordered an ultrasound. The ultrasound was performed, and I was told the baby was moving and had a strong heartbeat. I was hopeful again, thanking God and convincing myself that what was happening was completely treatable.

Following the ultrasound, I was transported to a room to wait for the physician's diagnosis. It was the longest wait of my life. My heart and my mind deliberated on whether my baby was, in fact, whole. My heart was beating abnormally loudly and incredibly fast. I was in a land I had never been before and desperately wanting to be rescued. The doctor came in approximately fifteen minutes after my ultrasound; her countenance was pleasant and agreeable. She pulled a chair adjacent to my bed, looked directly into my eyes, and said, "I'm sorry, you are going to miscarry. Go home. Rest and follow up with your doctor Monday morning." My entire body suddenly felt numb; I was in an immediate fog of disbelief. My joy and expectancy evaporated. The hospital room suddenly had no distinctive shape or color; everything displayed a grayish appearance. Several minutes after receiving the shocking news, I proceeded to get out of the bed. I stood up, and before me was a mirror on the wall, reflecting confusion and a weathered expression from the chaos in my mind. The news left me in a quandary. The stark reality of life and death being so close sent shivers down my spine. I felt sick to my stomach at the thought of not carrying my baby full term. I could not accept that truth. I asked others to pray, and I prayed fervently, placing all my confidence in God and standing firmly on my convictions.

I walked out of the hospital, got into my car, and drove home. While driving home, the echoing sound of the doctor saying I was going to miscarry tormented me. I had thoughts of ending it all, accompanied by specific visual images depicting how. At the time, it all seemed perfectly logical. But God . . . I arrived home and rested as advised. My husband and I prayed incessantly, day and night, hour after hour. We held onto hope. Sunday came. Although, meteorologically, it was a bright and sunny day, I could only see darkness. I was in a black hole, begging to be rescued, begging to be heard, but no one could hear or see me. I couldn't cry or climb my way out. I continued to pray as others prayed for me. I cried and begged for mercy to reign in my circumstance. My entire household was now pregnant with both terrifying ambiguity and unlikely hope.

Monday morning, my husband and I went to visit with my obstetrician. Another ultrasound was performed, a very brief one. The ultrasound technician simply said, "I'm sorry," and rushed out of the room. The doctor came in and confirmed the baby was already in the birth canal. My pregnancy was not viable. It was like a cruel blow. Every fiber of my being begged for mercy, my mind incredulously pleading for an alternative truth. To add insult to injury, my doctor communicated that I must go through the normal process of delivering my baby, whom I would not be taking home. The horror multiplied, and my heart began to swell up with anger. A wall was erected, even as I was being wheeled to the maternity ward. Lying on the hospital bed, waiting for the time to deliver, was the strangest feeling I have ever known; on one hand I was joyfully associating the moment to the three times I had previously brought forth life; on the other hand, I faced a grueling task that would yield no reward. I delivered a baby girl shortly after, whom my husband and I named Cherith Hope. She was perfectly and wonderfully created by her Master.

There are no words to express the depth of the heartache I experienced seeing the unfinished body of my baby. Any words seem disproportionate to the level of distress I experienced. After delivery, I was left to deal with a hurricane of emotions. The emotional pain of being prematurely separated from my daughter pulsated through my body with every single contraction of my beating heart. I wrestled with God. I could not accept the fact that He had all power to change the outcome of my situation, but He did not. I became angry at anyone who would mention His name. Nothing had ever shaken my faith like the loss of my daughter. I didn't know how I would continue living. I felt like I could not trust God anymore. How could He appoint such a tragedy in my life and leave me to bear the weight alone? I thought to myself. Although I knew the truth, I felt as though my mind was emptied of any goodness I had ever known. God was out of my reach; loving and trusting Him was suddenly risky. Growing up in the church, I have always heard that our faith as believers will be tested. I had never been tested. I am certain of this because a test of this magnitude forced me to determine why I should persevere. Losing my daughter was a painful realignment of my spiritual equilibrium as a believer. After my experience, I grew more and more distant in my relationship with the Lord in my heart. I didn't want to admit it to myself or anyone else, but God knew, and He was patient with me. I had never known what it is like to be comforted by a holy God until I lost my daughter. He ministered to my broken heart in ways that I could not begin to describe, holding me close even in my rebellion. I continued to seek His guidance by praying, reading the Word, and crying my pain to Him. Because of the sustaining power of God and the encouragement of my family and my friends, I held onto faith.

The week following my miscarriage, I made an appointment to meet with Christy, desperately needing help exploring my emotions. I wanted to cry my hurt to someone who I knew would listen and hold my hand while I honestly confessed what I was experiencing. I walked into Christy's office, unable to express any of what I was feeling. I told Christy, "I don't know why I'm here."

"Walk me through it," she said. With wisdom and overwhelming sympathy, she helped me produce the language to express my pain and disappointment. Christy prayed with me and specifically asked God to take away some of the mercies reserved for her and allow me to receive them. WOW! I bawled! During our conversation, God gave her a vision that would change all of my "Whys" to "How." I continuously asked God why he didn't save my baby, instead of how my suffering would all make sense, or how He would be glorified through it. We began talking about Come to the Garden, and Christy proposed the idea of choreographing an interpretive dance to the song "The Garden" by Kari Jobe. I had never heard the song before, and I certainly could not imagine actually accomplishing what Christy was requesting of me. Politely, I smiled and nodded at the idea, implying I agreed with her proposal, when in fact I was absolutely terrified at the thought. My mind was consumed with the overwhelming desire to hold my baby, and I was certainly not ready to surrender. Worshipful adoration to God seemed illogical. Following my meeting with Christy, I began studying the lyrics of the song and eventually added movement to the words. The song was now meaningful and relevant to me. I rehearsed tirelessly, expressing exactly what I felt with every word. I didn't know it then, but God was divinely, omnipotently transforming me. The song was now alive, not only in choreographed dance moves, but in my heart.

The Lord revealed His surpassing greatness at the retreat. While I was dancing to "The Garden," everything changed. I combined my pain with deliberate praise and worship to my God, and a deeper fellowship with God was kindled. As I lifted my worship, I felt as though I was trading my pain for unspeakable joy. Even with a broken heart, doubt, and fear, He received me; He embraced me and my pain. He loved me through my doubts and struggle to trust Him. Tragedy and grace collided, and His tangible presence filled the room as He healed not only my broken heart, but several others. Walls fell, chains broke. It was then I realized my pain had purpose. People yielded in admiration of my Savior. As I worshiped, others saw Him through my suffering, He healed hurts through my suffering, and He drew others close and revealed His love for them because of my suffering. God met me at Come to the Garden, and He gave me a new reason to worship Him and to fall deeper in love with Him.

Although I miss my daughter and would have wanted to see her grow up, I believe God's plan for me is greater. I will never fully understand why I had to go through this horrible experience; however, I do know that God is sovereign, and whatever He appoints to enter my life will always serve His divine purpose and will be used for my ultimate good. As I persevere, I know I will have moments of sadness and constant reprises of the day I said hello and goodbye simultaneously to my baby girl. However I trust in His holy capacity to carry me through. Eleven months later, He is already making all things beautiful. I am emboldened by the very circumstance that has shaken my faith and changed the trajectory of my life. I don't know what is ahead for me, but I'm securely wrapped in His arms as

I journey through this life. I am waiting with great anticipation for the day I will see my daughter again in unimaginable levels of joy and glory. Until then, the death and resurrection of my Lord Jesus is my consolation.

Chapter 7

Grow Up!

"The right manner of growth is to grow less in one's eyes."

—Thomas Watson

In part two of my dream, I pulled into the driveway a second time on a different day. The yard was still brown, but it was still clean! I was still filled with joy. There are two flowerbeds that are made with stones that go around two trees in the yard. Of course, in real life, nothing grows in them, because of those magnolia leaves. As I walked closer to the yard, I noticed something different about those beds. What??!! There were tiny green shoots coming up, and, not only that, there were tiny purple and yellow blooms growing! I wanted to do cartwheels across the yard and into the street! I said, "My God, my God! Thank you, thank you, thank you! Not only did you clean up my mess, but now there is life here!" Small as it was, it was absolutely thrilling to me. I felt like I could've died right there and I would have died happier than I've ever been. And God said, "Little girl" (He calls me that sometimes.), "Little girl, you're happy with Me cleaning up your mess and with this little bit of life. Honey, you ain't seen nothing yet." "That's great," I thought. "But would you look at this clean yard with little flowers growing in it? I can't take it in! Thank you, Jesus!"

On this night of the retreat, the sticks were gone. Replacing them were ivy and single blooms decorating the altar and the stage.

There is something that makes a plant grow. There is something in every plant life, whether a plant or a tree or a flower or a shrub. Plants and trees and flowers all have an ingredient called meristem, or sometimes it's referred to as the meristem line. The meristem line on every living plant or every living tree or every living flower is at the base of that tree, plant, or flower where it goes into the ground.

The meristem receives the nutrients, it then divides the nutrients, and then it causes part of that flower to grow up. And it says to other nutrients, "You need to go down." If you look closely enough at a plant or a tree, you can see the evidence of this. Sometimes it looks like a knot. If you were to cut the tree down and look at the bark, you would see a line that is a different color. This line is where a decision is made. This particular spot in the plant is where the plant takes what it's given, and then there's a decision made—whether what the plant has been given is going to go up or go down. It's where a decision is made to either go high or to go low. This decision is made at the meristem line.

What's very interesting is that this is similar to cells in our bodies. When a baby is forming, decisions are made at the stem cell line like: "You would make a good cell for the heart. You would make a good cell for the brain." Cells that don't get identified can become dangerous cells, and multiple unidentified cells can multiply into bad cells. Cells that are coming in and not put in the right place can cause cancer and other diseases.

What I want you to understand is simply this, this process is how the body handles what it's given. It's how the plant handles what it's given, how it determines if it's good or if it's bad. There is a decision that is made.

The plant doesn't have a lot to say about what nutrients that it's given, but it decides, "I'm going to let you grow me up," or, "I'm going to let you take me down." "I'm going to let you take me high" or, "I'm going to let you take me low." The plant or the tree makes that decision at the meristem line. The body makes that decision at the stem cell line. It's an amazing thing!

To the one we are an aroma that brings death; to the other, an aroma that brings life.

— 2 Corinthians 2:16(NIV)

In other words, the Gospel that is preached is an aroma or taste of life unto some and an aroma or taste of death to others. Another way to say that is that some people can hear the truth, hear the Gospel, and breathe in or take in life. And their life is blessed. Their families are blessed. They grow, and they get stronger in the Lord. Other people will hear the same truth, the same Gospel, and it does nothing for them.

You can have one person go through the most unspeakable of circumstances bitterly, yet have another go through identical circumstances in a transcendent way. It could be the loss of a child. It could be the loss of a marriage. It could be a bankruptcy. It could be a bad report from the doctor. It could be a financial disaster. It could be the discovery that a husband is having an affair. It could be any tough circumstances.

What is amazing is that some people will get bitter, but some people will get better. It's all according to what they do with what they take in. You can't choose everything that life is going to give you. It's not what happens to you; it's what happens in you that makes the difference. You are going to do something with the trials that you are going through. They can either take you up, or they can take you down. They can either cause you to bear fruit upward, or they can cause you to grow a root of bitterness downward.

None of us choose trials. You certainly didn't ask for that trial, but that is what life has given you, and God has allowed it. You have to make a decision at the spiritual meristem line of your soul. "I'm either going to let this take me up or take me down. It's either going to make me better, or it's going to make me bitter." This is a choice I have to make. This is a choice you have to make. Not God.

Problems will come. Trials will come. Tragedy will come. Hurdles will come. Circling the wilderness for too long, bringing the same burden, the same problem. I love what God says to the Israelites after they'd circled the wilderness for forty years.

> *Then God said, 'You've been going around in circles in these hills long enough; go north.'*
>
> — Deuteronomy 2:2 (MSG)

This is for someone: "You've been going around in circles long enough! Go NORTH!!" What decision will you make at the meristem line?

Lots of people go to church. Just because you go to church doesn't mean you're going to get anything out of it. What are you going to do with what life gives you? Are you going to send it up so it can bear fruit, or are you going to send it down where it will grow into a root of bitterness? Are you going to let it make you better and stronger, or are you going to let it make you bitter and weaker.

You will have countless chances to get bitter in life. Someone will hurt you. Someone will leave you. Someone will betray you. There will be disappointments. There will be injustices. And when that happens, at the spiritual meristem line of your soul, you make a decision.

Last night we read:

> *. . . by this root of bitterness, you defile many.*
>
> — Hebrews 12:15 (NKJV)

Your bitterness doesn't just affect you. It will affect your marriage. It will affect your children. It will affect your family. It will affect the world. You do realize they are watching us, don't you? The world watches as we go through a tragedy. They see one believer get bitter and spew it out in every conversation, and they can see another believer in that same situation bearing fruit. And as they scratch their head and ask how? Oh my, what an opportunity we have! That believer grows, and that believer goes deeper with God.

Trials can become a bad cancer cell to your soul, or you can take that same cell and say, "Nope, you'd make a good life-giving cell." You decide. You decide whether it becomes a good, life-giving cell, or whether it becomes a spiritual cancer cell to your soul.

And the remnant who have escaped of the house of Judah shall again take root downward, and bear fruit upward.
— Isaiah 37:31 (NKJV)

God said to the tribe of Judah, "The Assyrians are coming, and you are going to see them decimate My people." And then He said, "There's going to be a remnant, and out of that remnant will come fruit that will grow upward and roots that will grow downward."

There is a place in your soul, a spiritual meristem line where you make a decision to either let life cause you to grow bitter, or you let it produce the Fruit of the Spirit upward. What fruit is that?

Chapter 8

What Fruit is That?

But the fruit of the Spirit is love, joy, peace, long suffering, kindness, goodness, faithfulness, gentleness, self-control.

— Galatians 5:22 (NKJV)

God says, "If you'll trust Me with the trials and in the trials, if you'll choose to let them grow you up, I'll not let you just go through it and gain nothing out of it. Instead, I'll take you higher, and out of it, I'll grow things in you that you'll have trouble containing."

Instead of getting bitter and hateful and cynical and offended, you can let it grow you up and produce love, joy, peace, long suffering, kindness, goodness, faithfulness, gentleness, and self-control.

"You hurt me so badly, and I shouldn't turn around and bless you, but I'm not going to let it take me down. I'm going to let it grow me up, and I'm going to let it produce blooms and fruit!"

There's a place in God where we're supposed to do that. What we see above the ground is what we love, but what happens underneath the ground is what determines what happens above the ground. If your good root system is growing down, it's just a matter of time before you start bearing fruit up.

It takes one thousand hours of cold weather for a peach tree to bear fruit. South Carolina, where I moved from, grows amazing peaches. Florida does not. Florida has too much sunshine and too many warm days. South Carolina grows great peaches because there are plenty of cold-weather days. In order to produce the fruit of peach, you have to have at least one thousand hours of cold weather.

If you're interested in bearing fruit, then the Holy Spirit says, "Then there will have to be some cold days." Or, another way to put it:

"Storms make trees take deeper roots."

— Cabin 5

It's not enough to just come to church and have blessings, blessings and blessings, and more blessings. God will allow cold days into your life too, but it's out of the cold days that we grow and bear fruit upward!

Did you know that you can take any tree and turn it into a bonsai tree? It may be difficult with a palm tree, but you can use an oak tree, a pine tree. What happens when it starts growing? Nutrients are coming in at the meristem line. There are nutrients that are being sent up, and there are nutrients being sent down. The tree is growing both ways. But then, at a certain point, it's taken out of the box, and then shears are used to begin to cut the roots. And then it's put back into the box. They keep trimming the roots until the tree will just grow so high. Until it just won't grow anymore.

Now, the bonsai tree doesn't die. It's not that you're not saved. The bonsai just never grows. It never gets bigger. It never gets stronger. It just stays tiny and dwarfed. Satan just comes along and trims those roots and keeps you in a box. He keeps you where you've always been. That's why you find yourself coming to the altar with the same things over and over. That's why you feel no victory. Your good roots keep getting nipped and trimmed. You never get into the Word "because it's just not helping!" (snip, snip) You're believing that lie.

You are being deceived. The very lifeline that will free you, Satan convinces you it won't help, and so the purpose and destiny that is on your life lies dormant. God didn't give you life for you to be a bonsai tree.

The righteous shall flourish like a palm tree, He shall grow like a cedar in Lebanon. Those who are planted in the house of the Lord shall flourish in the courts of our God.

— Psalm 92:12-13 (NKJV)

They will flourish! They will be like one of the cedars of Lebanon! This could speak of your relationship with God. You're born again. You're headed to heaven. But this (bonsai tree) is not the end of your Christian walk! Jesus didn't bleed and die so that you could just be saved but never grow up and produce fruit. And never have roots of prayer. And never have roots of sowing. And never have roots of service.

It's the unseen parts of our lives that produces the outward fruit of our lives. Do you have a prayer life? Are you staying in the Word? Are you praising and worshiping? Are you saying "Thank You, Lord?" What is happening when you're not in fellowship with the body of Christ? What is happening when you're alone?

In Matthew, it says what we do in secret will be rewarded openly. That's why showboats don't typically have a lot of fruit growing on their trees. What you see is all you get. That's as deep as it is. Everything is public. Jesus said, "And that will be their only reward."

But what's happening under the ground, what's happening in our secret place, that's what causes us to grow up and grow out. In a good way!

The secret to a tall tree is the unseen roots. He said, "Judah, you're going to go through something." When life gives you trouble, when life gives you trials, you can either let it take you down, or you can let it grow you up—and bear fruit. But that's not God's decision. It's your decision.

I can't imagine the unthinkable heartache that may be represented by people reading this. Most of it I don't know. I wish you hadn't gotten the bad news. I wish those things hadn't happened to your family. I wish he hadn't left you. I wish you didn't have to fight through physical pain every day of your life.

But what are you going to do with it since that's part of life? You have to say, "I refuse to grow roots of bitterness. I will give this to God, and I will partner with Him in using my life for His purposes. I will let this be the fertilizer on my seed." As smelly as fertilizer is, as disgusting as it can be, as much as I hate to get near it, it's necessary for the growth process.

"But he is cruel to me. Christy, you have no idea what he says to me behind closed doors." No one is called to be a doormat to anyone, and Jesus never meant for any of his children to be abused. That's not what I'm talking about. What did Jesus do? He said, "Father, forgive them."

The devil has a lot of shears. Lots of scissors. He will do everything he can to stop you from growing up and bearing fruit. If he can cut you off at your good roots, then he has made you a dwarfed bonsai tree. Pretty to look at, for sure, but useless in every other way.

I certainly wasn't planning to go through a difficult separation that not only separated me from my husband, but separated me from my son. I certainly wasn't planning on starting a business, buying property for said business, only for a recession to come not long after. I certainly hadn't planned to watch my parents going through hell because my drug-addicted nephew was robbing them blind and putting them at risk from gangs in their area. I was going under. I was overwhelmed. But this is what I chose to do: I chose to fast. I chose to pray. I chose to take my mind off my circumstances and fix my eyes on what I know is Truth. Not the facts. The Truth.

Whatever life sends you, when it arrives, and it will, at your spiritual meristem line somewhere deep inside of your soul—when something happens that you weren't planning on, you have to make a decision. "This is not taking me down! God may have allowed it, so I will have to go through it, but I will allow the Holy Spirit to take it, and produce in me, through the cold days, fruit that I can't get any other way."

Let it develop you. Let it strengthen you. Don't get offended. You can stop life's blows. It's all in how you respond. There are two marks of a great person:

- They give.
- They are givers.

   I have never met a person, studied a person, read about a person who was great who was not a giver. They give. They give love. They give kindness. They give resources. They're givers.

If you want to be great, then give. The other mark of a great person is the they forgive. The only way you'll reach greatness in the Kingdom, is if you give, and you give, and you give. You give to the people who do you good, and you give to the people who do you harm. You give to those that you could crush. You give. You give. And you forgive. Those are the marks of greatness.

It's my attitude, not my achievements, that gives me happiness. The same sun that melts butter hardens clay. My heart can either harden or soften. I can either get clogged up with a bitter root, or I can grow up and bear fruit: Love, joy, peace, patience, kindness, goodness, faithfulness, gentleness and self-control. Or I can get mean and nasty and mad.

I can walk in love and joy and peace, or I can walk around a victim. I can choose death, or I can choose life. I don't know about you, but I must choose life. You can have two people going through the same thing and one gets better, and one gets bitter. It all happens at that spiritual meristem line. Where you say, "I didn't ask for this, but—"

Paul said:

> *For our light affliction, which is but for a moment, is working for us a far more exceeding and eternal weight of glory."*
>
> — 2 Corinthians 4:17 (NKJV)

> *. . . that Christ may dwell in your hearts through faith; that you, being rooted and grounded in love, may be able to comprehend with all the saints what is the width and length and depth and height — to know the love of Christ which passes knowledge; that you may be filled with all the fullness of God.*
>
> — Ephesians 3:17-19 (NKJV)

> *Now to Him who is able to do exceedingly abundantly above all that we ask or think.*
>
> — Ephesians 3:20 (NKJV)

Wait, we always stop there, but we must get the rest!

Now to Him who is able to do exceedingly abundantly above all that we must ask or think, according to the power that works IN US.

You mean God's exceeding power is waiting on the decision that I make at my spiritual meristem line? And, when I decide with the right attitude, what I'm going through is NOT going to take me down. It's going to take me up. I'm not going to grow roots of rejection and roots of abandonment. I'm not going to grow roots of offense. I'm not going to grow roots of rage. I'm not going to grow roots of depression. I'm not going to grow roots of bitterness toward people or toward God. No.

I'm going to grow up and grow fruit. He says, "I'll do exceedingly, abundantly, above all that you could ask or think, according to the power that works in you. What you are going through right now will either grow you up or take you down. The trial that you may be going through in your marriage will either take your marriage down or grow your marriage up.

God's Word to you today is, *"You will not grow if you allow the enemy to do what he wants to do through your trials. When you submit to God and say, 'Lord, I'm yours.' Then you will grow good roots downward."*

> *He is like a tree planted by water, that sends out its roots by the stream, and does not fear when heat comes, for its leaves remain green, and is not anxious in the year of drought, for it does not cease to bear fruit.*
>
> — Jeremiah 17:8 (ESV)

A previous retreat that we had was called Come to the River, and I hope we are living in the River, because where the River flows, EVERYTHING will live. Like a tree planted by the water. It will not be moved, and you will grow fruit upward.

There's another tree, the family tree. What is your family tree of faith like? The enemy doesn't care if you're saved, but he definitely doesn't want any of your children to be connected to your salvation. However, when you allow it, Jesus will take your roots downward and your fruit upward. When He does, it will not just affect one generation. It will affect your children and your children's children. As well as your children's children's children.

When my husband left me, he took my thirteen-year-old son with him. It was months before I knew where they were living. But, the night they left, I was on the floor of my bedroom screaming and sobbing. It felt like someone had died. My eleven-year-old daughter had to watch this. Neither of us slept that night. I took her to school the next day pale and with circles under her eyes. At work, I couldn't even function. I sat at my desk paralyzed. Not knowing what else to do, I turned on my computer and opened up my email. There was an email from a lady named Deloris. The email said this, "Christy, you don't know me, but I sing in the choir with you. I couldn't sleep at all last night. The Lord put you on my heart. I've been in so much pain and spiritual torment that I've begged the Lord to remove it. All I knew to do was to open my Bible. I came upon this Scripture. I'm not sure if it will mean anything to you or not, but I must give it to you."

This is the Scripture:

> *Thus says the Lord: Refrain your voice from weeping, And your eyes from tears; For your work shall be rewarded, says the Lord, And they shall come back from the land of the enemy. There is hope in your future, says the Lord, That your children shall come back to their own border.*
>
> — Jeremiah 31:16-17 (NKJV)

My roots went downward, my fruit grew upward. The circumstances didn't change at first. It took time, but I let God take my roots downward, and my fruit grew upward:

Peace

I rested at night because God had already made a promise that they would return.

Joy

I appreciated the little things like a response or a visit, and they became so precious.

Love

I was able to pray for my ex, the one who had wronged me, until I really meant it.

Faithfulness

I did what I could do and trusted God with the rest, continuing to remove the dead things, keeping the dirt tilled. I didn't let it get hard, but kept pulling up the bad roots and watering the good roots, planting God's Word seed by seed, DEEP, and taking all the pain, the disappointment, the fears, and fertilizing.

Patience

Day after day, month after month, year after year, with such slow growth.

My son questioned if there was a God. Some of your seeds that you planted have to do with your children. He who began a good work in you and your children will be faithful to complete it. I want us to make a declaration today: I want you to lift your hands toward heaven and say, "Lord, the stuff that's coming at me, I'm going to make a decision. I'm going to have an attitude adjustment. It's not going to take me down. I'm going to bear fruit upward. It's going to cause me to go higher. You've given me deep roots so that I can go higher and bear fruit in Jesus' name." (At the time of this writing, my son and I could not be closer, and he believes and serves our faithful God.)

There is no doubt in my mind that I am talking to people right now who never dreamed you would be where you are, going through what you're going through. This is a Word in season for your life. It doesn't have to take you into bitterness and anger and hopelessness. This same situation that will cause one to go down can cause you to go up and bear much fruit.

Romans 8 says that, *All things work together for good to them that are called according to His purpose.* Jesus never comes where He's not invited. If you've never invited Him, today is the day.

Some of you are at a crossroads. God has spoken to you. You know He's spoken to you. You feel the nudging. You feel the tugging. You may have had a knot in your throat as you read this. You have to make a decision. I can't make it for you. God won't make it for you. You have to decide at your spiritual meristem line. Aren't you tired? Aren't you so tired of circling these hills?

Decide today. Make a decision that you will not let these circumstances take you down, not one more minute. Make a decision, once and for all, that you will let what life has dealt you to take you up and to bear good fruit.

For many days I noticed my neighbor in his yard taking meticulous care of his flowers. He would literally hold one leaf or one petal and spray water on it. He had a yard full of plants and flowers, but he seemed to be interested in only the one. I wondered, why is he taking so much time with just the one? And God showed me. He is The Gardener. And that's how He cares for us. He prunes us individually. He breaks up the hard ground in us. He waters us and gives us just what we need uniquely.

Aren't you tired? Aren't you so tired of circling these hills? Decide tonight. Make a decision that you will not let these circumstances take you down, not one more minute. Make a decision tonight, once and for all, that you will let what life has dealt you to take you up and to bear good fruit. Ask God what word does He have for you today. Is it "growing in grace?" Or perhaps "redeemed?" I expect the word He has for you is the opposite of the lies you've been told in your life. He has broken the fallow ground in your heart. He has removed the roots that need to be removed. Now it's time for the seeds that have been planted to grow.

Chapter 9

Heather

You can't appreciate what happened at the garden until you understand where I've been. It started with a simple text request to my three best friends — "Give me one reason why I should see the 'forest from the trees' and care enough to keep trying," Trying to remain patient with whatever God's timing may have been. Trying to understand what my purpose in life was. Trying to feel like my life was headed in some discernible direction. It was the spring of 2014, and I had been cruising along and doing fine for a while. In the year prior, I had lost a great deal of weight, was a full-time student knocking out a 4.0, was living in a wonderful condo with a dear friend and mentor, had grown leaps and bounds in my spiritual life, and was the happiest and healthiest I had been in my adult life. And then nothing happened. I thought—well, I don't know what I thought. Perhaps that finally doing everything right meant God would deliver my dream life to me wrapped in a perfect, velvet bow. After all, when you're "livin' right," you're bound to be #blessed—or so says the prosperity gospel.

But, it didn't happen. I didn't receive any offers of marriage, and my belly didn't suddenly swell with successive children, enough to form my own little league team. So, I texted the three most important people in my life, desperate for someone to give me a reason. Yet nothing happened. No answer came. No three flashing dots on the screen of my iPhone indicating that an answer would be forthcoming. Nothing. Silence. A silence that I breathed in, but never breathed back out.

Thus began a three-year downward spiral into an immersion of depression, a disconnection from friends and family, and a day-to-day quest just to find a reason for existing. Roots of bitterness grew down and deep into a twisted infrastructure large enough to house the entirety of *Fraggle Rock*. The roots of bitterness broke ground at the end of 2016 and grew into a fully-grown oak of disappointment when, over the course of one weekend, I quit my job, dropped out of school, and buried myself under a pile of Valium, refusing to interact with anyone, least of all, God. In a moment of complete desperation, I sought Christian counseling. Progress came, little by little, until God's perfect timing allowed me to understand the Spirit of Pride that had started it all when He met me at the garden.

Pride brought an end to the complete perfection and harmony of heaven; taking down an entitled, legalistic, and judgmental human was alarmingly simple. Through counseling, I began to make progress, but a true breakthrough was elusive, until I agreed to show up by attending the River Dwellers weekly discipleship class.

Just about the time the River Dwellers' messages became more relevant and started getting all up into my business and personal space — when I would normally retreat — I was recruited to help with some of the technical aspects of the class, mainly, utilizing ProPresenter to display song lyrics and Scripture references on video screens. My help was further requested at the Come to the Garden retreat.

By the time the retreat rolled around, I had no desire to come to anyone's garden, much less one filled with enough estrogen to make me want to start doing arts and crafts in the shape of female body parts or singing "Kumbaya" with instruments fashioned from ribbons and whittled from beach wood. This is what I imagined a "Women's Retreat" to be. But, due to my position at River Dwellers, I felt I should go. I decided that if I had to be there, I would attend on my own terms. I booked an off-site room with a full kitchen so I could avoid being there for all but the essential times and overbooked myself with work so I'd have to spend the entire time working and completely absent from anything that resembled a time of fellowship or interaction with other human beings. Not even the allure of reliving my childhood by careening down a hill on an adult-sized Slip-N-Slide could entice me into participating beyond my dedicated time of service.

By the final night, I had managed to stay patronizingly distant and disconnected, avoided as many hugs as I could, and was knocking it out of the park with my ProPresenter kung-fu. And then I walked into the garden. Like, a literal garden that the ministry team had created in the worship center. Every vertical and horizontal space was covered in trees, plants, vines, ivy, leaves, and anything else you'd find in the Dowager Crawley's award winning English Garden. And Satan was all. Over. That. It was gorgeous, beautiful, amazing, phenomenal— and I had nothing to do with it, so, of course, I had to criticize and find problems with it.

My cynicism game is strong, and, when combined with my self-proclaimed comedic brilliance, I can deliver a barb that won't just hurt, it will scar. Pride, party of one, your table is ready! I was done. Done with being around these women with their pink shirts and their manicured fingernails and their Beth Moore "girlfriend" nicknames and their Lularoe Leggings and their essential oils and everything I wish I could be but know that I am not. Done. Done. Done. I started working on formatting the lyrics and setting up Scripture slides, and I received the message outline from our leader and weekend speaker, Christy Sawyer.

Title: *"It's Time to Grow Up!"* Well played, God, well played. I usually review the whole outline as a sort of dry run to be sure I have the correct version of the verses and picture/video cues. I made it to the third page and the citing of Deuteronomy 2:2, and that's where I stopped. I knew that verse. I knew that verse intimately. Deeply. Extensively. And a lot of other adverbs. God had given me that verse repeatedly over the past two years, through times of struggle and times of wellness. I didn't want to read any more, and I certainly didn't want to hear anymore. Cue: The Holy Spirit About to Jack Me Up.

Service started—I attempted to get the Facebook Live video rolling (to broadcast all the messages for those who could not attend and anyone else to watch in the future), and it was wrong. I then tried to redo it not once, not twice, but three times, and they were all wrong. Thankfully, one of the amazing FSOD young ladies was right there and able to get it figured out and running correctly, but the spiral had started. In the span of two minutes, the enemy had me fully convinced that Christy and her husband, Pastor Jonathan Sawyer, would never speak to me again, that everything Christy had planned for documenting that weekend was now destroyed, and that I was single-handedly responsible for ruining the Christy Sawyer Ministries big kick-off event. That's some serious pride. That's like Mufasa, from *The Lion King*, explaining to Simba how their land is called Pride Rock, but then I show up with a real estate development sign and declare it Heather Rock instead. It took everything in me not to bolt. Christy came and sat next to me during worship, and the enemy began whispering made-up thoughts that he convinced me had to be what she was thinking—"I ask one thing of her, and she screws it up," "I should have given it to an FSOD girl in the first place," and "Shoot, I could have given it to a well trained border collie, and it would have been done right." That's when the tears began. I was sitting there with Operation Destroy All Emotional and Spiritual Progress going on in my head and tears and snot streaming down my face when Christy began speaking. I began trying to calm myself by building up those walls God had been breaking down the past few months in counseling.

Then she gets to the part of the outline involving Deuteronomy 2:2, which references the Israelites circling the desert for years, and she says, "This Scripture is for somebody here tonight. Listen: Then God said, 'You have been going around in circles long enough! ENOUGH! GO NORTH!!! GO NORTH!!!' My heart breaks for you! God never meant you to live this way. Never!'"

Her emotions were coming through strong, and her voice broke.

And then the Holy Spirit broke me. I collapsed into the ugly cry as though Oprah was interviewing me. Snot bubbles began floating away towards the back row. I moved into hiccups and face contortions. Maureen (a lovely lady helping with some of the videotaping) looked like she didn't know if she should pat me on the back, start performing an exorcism, or call Medic Alert. I honestly have no idea how the Scripture slides made it up on the screen except through divine intervention. I finally calmed down into regular "I'm watching a Nicholas Sparks movie" sniffles right about the time that she decided to pull out a scene (which happens to be my favorite scene) from the book *Redeeming Love* (which happens to be my favorite book). Oh, it's like that, is it? Low blow, low blow! At that point, Maureen had on a life vest and was in a makeshift boat made from a cardboard box and an extra wood pallet, rowing around in the river of my tears and snot. Throughout the sermon, she'd been graciously and lovingly bringing me huge batches of paper towels from the bathroom. They were roughly the consistency of #4 Sandpaper, but I didn't care. I just keep blowing through them and stuffing them into a bag I won in a raffle. By the time the message was finished, it was overflowing to the point of needing to be disposed of in a contractor's garbage bag, I couldn't breathe out of either nostril, and my head was pounding.

I spent the entire altar call with my head in my hands, still sobbing, and letting it all go, one prideful thought at a time. All that I'd been holding onto through years of circling the desert—years of putting my worth in the hands of others, years of denying myself freedom from pride, and years of allowing pride to bind me and destroy what God wanted for me. Two lovely friends each took turns comforting me—one through prayer and one just by calmly letting me know she was there and supporting me. Maureen hugged me and told me over and over how much she loved me.

The enemy started redoubling his efforts, but at that point, I ain't playin' anymore. Every thought he threw at me, I took captive. Every doubt he tried, I stamped out. I like to think that I was spiritually knocking Satan on his rear. Since I'll never be athletic enough to head kick anyone taller than 2'4", I like having a mental picture of me roundhouse drop kicking the Prince of Darkness right in the face while the theme to Walker, Texas Ranger plays in the background. At the end of the altar call, we were told that there were 150 ceramic flowers up front. Each had been prayed over. Each had a phrase and verse on the bottom. We were instructed to, when led, come up front and choose one without looking at whatever may be written for us on the bottom.

Eventually, I pulled myself together enough to crawl to the altar and choose my flower. I should have known. I should have picked up on the pattern of the night and realized what was coming. But, of course, God had to show off. Again.

Once I returned to my seat, I turned it over to read: "Go Forth! Isaiah 49:9." When read together, it says, *Go forth . . . to say to the captives, 'Come out,' and to those in darkness, 'Be free!'* More wailing and gnashing of teeth, and I finally got myself back to my hotel. Physically, I was miserable and a mess. Emotionally, I was a wreck. Spiritually, I was in battle.

The following morning's message was the perfect end cap and propelling force to what God had started the night before. All the things God wants of me, even if I don't know what He has for me, were reinforced. All the dreams I'd given up on and the daily attempts I'd made for the past few years to squash those dreams so I wouldn't have to be disappointed anymore, were reignited—first and foremost being my love of writing and telling stories.

I have had YEARS of circling this same issue of pride as my desert, and I know what it's caused me to do to myself physically (Prednisone addiction, anyone?), emotionally (living like a hermit to avoid an emotional connection with anyone), and spiritually. I know the love I have for a man I may not have even met yet (or maybe I have?).

The entire drive home from that retreat, God was speaking to me. Constantly. And He hasn't stopped since. He's giving me...messages. I don't know what else to call them. Not messages as in the tin-foil-hat-wearing kind that are delivered to true believers in double-wide trailers about the potential existence of aliens or whether Elvis may or may not still be alive, but messages. Of hope. Encouragement. Struggles. Triumphs. And everything in between—the vehicle of which is yet to be determined. Right now, I feel no call to directly seek the lost. I feel called to those like me.

I arrived home after my two-hour drive with an entire series of discipleship messages and a hunger to get it out there. Within an hour of being home, I received a message from a family friend I hadn't spoken to in over ten years. Her message simply asked if I'd ever thought about writing and publishing, that she knew someone who could get me in touch with Christian writers, and I should let her know if I was interested. It took me a lot longer to respond than it should have, but it's a little difficult to form a coherent thought, much less response, when you're yelling, "Are you kidding me?!?!?" at your ceiling. Her next response included an invitation to one of the largest Christian writers' conferences where I could be introduced to agents, writers, and publishers. And that's literally what my life has been since the retreat. A nonstop outpouring of opportunity right in line with what God has asked of, and given, me—a call I'd never thought I'd have. It didn't happen because I got my act together or worked tirelessly to become a snowy, white paragon of Christianity or filled with self-righteous, holiness living.

It happened because I was willing to show up to a discipleship class and an out-of-my-comfort-zone retreat. God met me there and did the rest.

Chapter 10

Arise My Love

"Why fit in when you were born to stand out?"

— Dr. Seuss

On the final day of the retreat, when the ladies walked into the worship center, there were gasps, there were tears and there were giggles of delight. The entire space had been transformed into a wild and beautiful garden. Not just the stage and the altar, but down the rows, all of it. It was filled with plants and flowers and trees. The stage and the altar were literally dripping in blooms. Before I even saw it (I was still in my room putting finishing touches on the message I was to deliver), Tiffany, who is on my ministry team and in charge of making everything we do beautiful, called me in tears. She told me that even in the process of putting it all together, she and her volunteers felt the Holy Spirit so powerfully. She told me that she felt like she, herself, had been transported into my dream. Needless to say, when I walked in there myself, I was overwhelmed. I expected it to be beautiful, but this—this was anointed. I already knew that the events before the dream to all these years later were God-ordained—for this retreat—and I knew all the events to occur; all of it was interwoven into a bigger plan that involved His daughters everywhere. But for me, for Christy, in that moment, it was just me and Him. It was Him smiling at me and saying, "I told you." Yes, it was a room full of rented plants and flowers, but it was so much more than that. It was a visual that had progressed through the weekend that women could see themselves in God's plan and process. It was completion.

This, of course, represented the final part of my dream. I was already in the old house. I came out on the front porch and couldn't believe my eyes. There was about an acre, a perfect rectangle (in reality, the yard is much smaller) that I knew was mine. Filling the borders was the most luscious, green, jungle-like scene, yet in perfect order. There were paths all through it. It was wild but it wasn't chaotic at all. And in the center was a gazebo. The "center," the gazebo, was calling for me. I thought I would lose my mind at the wonder of it all. I walked down the steps of my front porch and began to walk through this wild, green wonderful place. And with every step I took, the green things would bloom as I walked by. And the colors! These weren't colors that you find in a Crayola box. These were colors I had never seen before. There are no words to describe how I felt. When I woke, I knew that this dream was significant and that it was from the Lord. Flowers—the flowers in my dream represented women everywhere. And the colors were so different, so unique, just like the calling that is on every daughter's life. Your calling is like a snowflake, not any two are the same.

> *Arise, shine; for your light has come! And the glory of the Lord is risen upon you. For behold, the darkness shall cover the earth, and deep darkness the people; but the Lord will arise over you, and His glory will be seen upon you. The lost shall come to your light, and kings to the brightness of your rising. 'Lift up your eyes all around and see: They all gather together, they come to you; your sons shall come from afar, and your daughters shall be nursed at you side. We have had our dead things removed.'*
>
> — Isaiah 60:1-4 (NIV)

Our barren, dry and hard ground is being broken up. We have given God our roots of bitterness. We have planted our seeds of His promises and His Word deep into our watered and fertilized hearts. And today, God says to His daughters: *"Arise, My Love. Arise, shine! For your light has come. And the glory of the Lord is risen upon you!"* In other words, "Stand up and stand out."

God tells us in this Word, "I do not want My daughters, I do not want My church, to be hidden in a closet. Nor do I want you, My Beloved, to hide the light that is in you." God has put a light in each of you that the world is longing to see. There is a spirit of excellence on each of your lives, and the world responds to excellence.

How do you walk in that spirit of excellence? There are two ways:

1) Do what you do well.

2) Do what you do well, with a good attitude.

If you do what you do well, and you do it with a good attitude, the light that God has put in you, the spirit of excellence, will begin to shine through you. In a dark world, you will stand up, and you will stand out.

Performance does matter. Your performance determines your platform. Your performance on your job, your performance where you volunteer, your performance in your school, determines the platform that you will have. Another way of saying platform is influence—influence that you will have among people.

When I say your performance will determine your platform, it means that people will listen to you based on your performance. Look at any well-known business person. Look at any successful athlete. If you look at any field in life that you want to use as an example, those with influence have all performed with excellence at their jobs. They have influence and a platform that other people do not have.

When you see people at the top of their field, nobody stops them from talking about Jesus Christ. When they win or when they achieve great things or receive awards, no one pulls the microphone away from them when they say, "First of all, I want to thank Jesus Christ."

There's something about their performance that determines their platform. When people are successful, when they win, the world wants to know how they did it. No one ever asked a person who settles for mediocrity or less in what they do, "How do you do it?" If you play basketball, and you miss the shot or lose the playoff game and fail at what you're doing, no one wants to know what your secret is.

In our Christian walk, we have some who walk around defeated all the time, still with a victim mind-set, and have others who walk around as overcomers. As was mentioned in a previous chapter, there are some who have gotten bitter with what life has given them, and then someone else, in the exact same circumstances, has gotten better through what life has given them. Both of these people are saved and headed to heaven, but one has influence, and the other one doesn't.

When you arise and shine, when you begin to stand up and stand out, it gives you influence with people. The one who is bitter is going to go to heaven; they're just not taking anyone with them. But the one who is better, the one who does what they do with influence, the one who has let the Lord take their roots downward and their fruit upward, is going to use that platform of excellence to influence a lot of people to go to heaven.

If you want to influence people, you have to bear fruit, and you have to become excellent at what you do. You're going to have to arise and shine. You're going to have to stand up and stand out, and when you stand up and stand out and you arise and you shine, God will begin to shine light into a dark world through you, and people will be drawn to you.

We must do what we do, well. If you work in an office, be the best employee, be the most reliable employee, on that job. It matters. That's what standing up and standing out is all about. If you're the one who's always late, if you're the one whose work is sloppy or your work never gets done, if you're not dependable, or if you're the one no one can ever get along with, then you're not going to have influence.

Some churches, some people, and actually some pastors have a terrible reputation in their communities. They're known for not paying their bills. Their facilities are not fresh and clean. They don't have a spirit of excellence.

When I think of a spirit of excellence, I think of my husband. He holds himself, his musicians, and his choir to a high standard of excellence. This has given him such a platform, such influence on the world around him. We've been in churches where you would have people get up to sing, and say, "Y'all pray for me. I didn't have any time to practice, so I need y'all to stretch your hands this way, 'cause I need a touch from the Lord." WHAT? You are representing our Lord with that?

Sloppiness in the body of Christ needs to come to an end. All of us need to have a spirit of excellence. The people in the Bible who influenced their generations were people of excellence. Think about David. The Bible said that David played his harp skillfully. He wasn't a giant slayer first. He wasn't a famous king first. He was a musician who was excellent at what he did.

Notice it didn't say he played a musical instrument. It said he played skillfully. Because he played skillfully, he began to rise and shine. He began to stand up and stand out with a musical instrument. The king heard about his skill and brought him into the palace because he had a spirit of excellence. It took him hours and hours and hours to become skillful at playing that musical instrument. That excellence was the thing that God used to get spiritual power into that palace and into that kingdom. Eventually that same spirit of excellence got David to the throne. Not only did David play skillfully and God used his spirit of excellence to impact multitudes, but he also influenced multitudes for generations. It all started with him becoming excellent at strumming a harp.

And then there's Daniel. You know what key characteristic of Daniel is talked about first? The Bible said he had an excellent spirit. In other words, he had an excellent attitude. We know he refused to eat the king's meat. He really had a standard. The thing that is the most impressive about that story is that when he and the other men wouldn't eat what the king offered, the Bible said when they came in ten days later, "their countenance was fairer, they were smarter and quicker, and sharper than the king's men. And they were ten times wiser."

The world and the king were drawn to them first in a natural way—because they were sharper. If they had been just like everyone else, doing just enough, if they had always had scowls on their faces and they showed up for work late every day and were the first to leave every day, this would not have been the case. The Bible said they were sharper. They were quicker than the king's men. The purpose of them taking the stand that they took was to prove that they could do more with God than with the king. They were quicker, wiser, sharper, and their excellence put them in a position in a heathen nation of influence and power, all because they did what they did well and with excellence.

And there's Joseph. The Bible says that God was with Joseph and that he prospered in every place. He was put in jail, and Joseph became the head of the jail. He was put in Potiphar's house as a slave, and Potiphar put him over everything in his household. It didn't matter where he was. He did everything with a spirit of excellence.

Some people will say, "If someone will just give me a break!" Listen, if you can't do it where you are, you won't do it anywhere else. You can arise and shine right where you are. This principle of doing well where you are with what you have works every time. I don't care what you do and where you do it. When you do it well and do it with excellence, you'll begin to stand up and stand out. Excellence will cause God's hand of promotion to come upon your life.

The Bible says that Joseph always did whatever he did with excellence. Everything he did prospered. Joseph's authority and influence got bigger and bigger and bigger. People who were in higher authority always wanted Joseph close to them. That's the power of excellence. If you will become excellent, people with authority will want you close to them. They will pull you in. You will stand out of the herd. They will start asking your opinion because there is a spirit of excellence on you. This always happens. It's a law in the Kingdom.

If you want to have favor with people of authority, and I'm not just talking about saved people—most people don't care if you're saved or not—do your job with excellence. They don't hire you to speak in tongues and quote Bible verses all day long. They hire you do to an excellent job. If you shine on your job, those people are going to pull you in close to them be- cause people of authority are ALWAYS drawn to people of excellence. Every time.

You can give someone all the Scripture you want, but if they come near you and all they hear is about how you've been done wrong again, if all they see are bitter roots sticking out of you and no fruit on your tree, if you're asking to borrow money again, because you refuse to balance your checkbook and stick to a budget, yet you're representing the kingdom? There's something wrong with that picture. That's not excellence. That's not standing up and standing out.

But when they see that you are the first one who arrives and the last to leave, when they see that they don't have to worry about your work getting done, when they see they can trust you with their resources, when they see the fruit of love, and kindness and patience and self-control, when they see the joy of the Lord in your countenance, when they can say that they've never heard you trash-talking anyone—I can guarantee you that people in authority will notice, and they will raise you up every time.

In 1 Kings the Bible says that the Queen of Sheba came from halfway around the world to see King Solomon's house that he had built, his personal house, the kingdom, and the temple that he had built. The Bible said that the thing that caused the Queen of Sheba to come, the thing that so astonished her, was when she noticed how happy King Solomon's servants were. To put it another way, when she saw how enthusiastic his employees were and when she saw the joy they had in their service, she was amazed. The Bible even mentions their attire, how clean and how sharp they were.

She saw how happy and enthusiastic the employees were, and Scripture says she saw the building he had built.

Through wisdom a house is built.

— Proverbs 24:3 (NIV)

Wisdom builds a house. How wise are you? And I'm not talking about the square footage of the house. I'm talking about those under your authority. How are they doing? Wisdom builds a house, and the people under your covering prosper if you're building it wisely —your children, not that they won't go through things, but if you build that house wisely, whoever is under that house is going to do well eventually because you keep praying and leading them in truth.

The LAST thing that the Queen of Sheba saw was Solomon's ascent to the throne of God. The first thing she saw was the grounds and the buildings and the servants, how sharp they were and how friendly they were, how classy they were and how excellent they were, how enthusiastic and happy and joyful and helpful they were.

We want to make it so spiritual, fighting demons and all of that. Maybe we just need to be kind to people. Maybe we just need to smile for a change. It would be amazing how God would cause your light to start influencing people, as you just arise and shine in a dark world. There has to be something that gives you the right and the authority to be listened to, and because Solomon met her in the natural world first, his performance gave him a platform.

Not everyone could reach the Queen of Sheba. She had it all. There are people in the marketplace. There are people in our schools. There are people in your neighborhoods that someone like me will NEVER reach. But there are people reading this, if you arise and shine, if you will stand up and stand out, if you will do well and with excellence what you've been given right this moment, you can reach them. They don't care about a preacher, but they are watching you. How are you handling what life has handed you? How do you speak on the job? How do you treat your family? How do you speak about your children and your husband? Their marriage may be falling apart. They may be making millions of dollars and may be in authority, but them seeing you doing it right it could change everything.

The Bible said THEN she came and she asked Solomon "the hard questions." Isn't that something? Once she saw his performance, it gave him platform. He didn't have to chase her with a Bible and say, "You need to get saved." He did what he did. His business did what it did, and the Bible said, "THEN she started asking him the hard questions."

"How do you keep your marriage together?" "My husband had a bad report from the doctor. I'm not a religious woman but I notice there's something different about you." "I don't know how to ask this, but would you pray for me?" "Would you ask the man upstairs to help my husband?"

They'll start asking you the hard questions. You don't earn the right to be listened to because of your failures. You earn the right to be listened to because of your successes. The Queen of Sheba couldn't be reached by just anyone. If she would have shown up at Solomon's house and there were pitiful, broken down weeds everywhere in the flower beds, if the employees didn't smile at her and didn't show hospitality, or if she'd have shown up and the place was filthy and everyone was unkempt and standing around with attitudes, think about what would have happened. If there were pieces of trash that hadn't been picked up, and if everyone was standing outside taking a cigarette break, flipping their butts on the ground, you get me? This stuff matters! No glory—no joy. I promise you, if this is what she would have seen, she wouldn't have asked the hard questions.

It's time to arise and shine. It's time to stand up and stand out. The Bible says when you become excellent at something, the lost will come to your light and the brightness of your promotion or your rising. God wants to raise people up in the marketplace. God wants to raise people up in our schools. God wants to raise people up in our government. God wants to raise people up in our churches. He wants to raise you up in your field.

Whether you clean houses for a living, whether you're a waitress, a secretary, a student, a teacher, a volunteer, or a business owner, the cry of your heart should be: "God, I want to stand up and stand out. I want to arise and shine. Give me a spirit of excellence. God, I want my light to shine in a dark world, so that people will be drawn to You. I can tell them my secret, now that they are asking me. I didn't chase them down and badger them and pound them on the head with my Bible. I didn't have to leave index cards on their desks with

Scriptures on them. They started asking me the hard questions." That's when you know your light is shining wherever you are.

I think it's interesting that when God sent His son to the earth, He didn't place Him in a priest's home. If that had been me, if I was going to send my son to redeem the world, I would have put him in a religious atmosphere. I would have sent him to a third-generation Pentecostal family. God didn't do that. God put him in a marketplace environment. God put him in an environment where He learned a trade, and He learned it skillfully. God allowed Him until He was thirty years old to deal with orders and billing and work with stone and lumber and deal with customers. For thirty years He never preached a sermon. What did He do? He worked.

This is an hour when we have enough crosses in the church. Jesus dragged His cross down the Via Dolorosa which was straight down the business district of Jerusalem. He didn't take a back road. He took His cross right in the middle of the secular world. We don't have to literally drag a cross where we are planted. You just do what you do and do it well. Arise and shine. Stand up and stand out. Be excellent in what you do, and be excellent in your attitude. When you do, your light will shine. Matthew 5 says, "You will be the light of the world." When are we going to understand that the people we are around all day don't care who our preacher is or what church we go to. They may not be reading the Bible, BUT THEY ARE READING YOU!

Some of you need a change in your life. First of all, Jesus needs to be the Lord of your life. God has given you a dream, and His Word to you today is, "Arise and Shine." Stand up and stand out. Begin with excellence, but it all has to be built on Jesus Christ. If you get in His will, He WILL exalt you. If you apply this principle of doing even the small things with excellence, it will work every time. He is no respecter of persons.

Arise, shine; for your light has come! And the glory of the Lord is risen upon you. For behold, the darkness shall cover the earth, and deep darkness the people; but the Lord will arise over you, and His glory will be seen upon you.

— Isaiah 60:1-4 (NIV)

When we put a seed in the ground, we have to let it go, and what we've sown in tears, we will reap in years. The time of mourning is over. God has replaced our mourning with a garment of praise. You have let go of some things; you have surrendered things to the Lord. You have planted seeds that have been watered by your tears, and God will be faithful to grow those seeds up into fruit-bearing trees. Arise, shine; for your light has come! And the glory of the Lord is risen upon you.

Chapter 11

Lisa

My garden story began about a year before the Come to the Garden retreat was held. As I was preparing to do the head table for our church's annual women's missions tea, I reached into a cabinet to get some dishes, and as I moved aside a paper bag of some unused plates, God simply said to me "The Garden." With those two words, I knew right then and there that He was already calling me to do the next year's missions tea and the theme was to be The Garden.

Seems like a simple enough directive, but for me, it was huge. I was just stepping back into the tea after losing our youngest son, Jordan, and his two best friends, Jon and Joe, in a horrific car accident. Jordan was only eighteen years old and had just graduated from high school. He had simply gone out to dinner with his friends and never came home. It was a huge step of faith getting back into the tea, still early in my grief journey, and here God was already showing me the table for the next year with The Garden as the theme.

In the meantime, even though I wasn't putting it all together yet, I began doing my daily devotions out on our back porch and started a container garden. I hadn't gardened since Jordan and I had used to plant rose bushes together, but I found the whole process to be so ministering, nurturing and healing to me. During my devotional time on our porch, I discovered Kari Jobe's new single "The Garden" and began playing the song over and over again. When Kari released the full album, and I saw the cover, I immediately saw what the missions tea table was to look like. Her album matched the very plates over which God had spoken "The Garden" to me.

While looking to pull up "*The Garden*" song one morning on YouTube, I discovered an interview with Kari Jobe and her husband about the story behind The Garden. I learned Kari had written The Garden song while she and her family were grieving the loss of her sister's baby. It was then that I began to realize that the Lord hadn't just spoken The Garden to me to do the missions tea. He was using His garden to speak hope to my broken heart over the loss of my boy. I just had no idea at the time how large and far His garden would grow.

My husband and I own two women's retail stores, and while we function as a marketplace ministry on a daily basis, each spring for the past twelve years, we have had a truly God breathed ministry called Women of Worth! After pushing back all of our clothing racks and dis- plays and setting up chairs on a Friday night, we have as many as 150 women gather at our retail store early on a Saturday morning for our WOW! sessions. We bring in a guest speaker, serve breakfast, have ministry in song, and give away fun prizes. A few months after God had spoken The Garden to me, Christy Sawyer "happened" to be our guest speaker at WOW! After the session when we were chatting, Christy asked me if I was coming to her retreat in the fall. I told her that I had hoped to be able to attend if I could arrange my schedule. She then asked me, "Do you know the name of the retreat?" When she told me "Come to the Garden," I can't even imagine what my face looked like. I know my mouth fell open, and I felt like I was about to fall to the floor!

Yet, despite that divine set-up, I was still struggling with how I was going to be able to go to retreat with my demanding schedule during the fourth quarter of retail. The Lord knows us so well, though, and knew what it would take to get me there. He gave me an idea to have a table for us to sell some of our store's garden-themed products at the retreat, with all the profits going to Christy's ministry. My com- mitment to doing the table locked me into being at retreat.

If you remember, I had already been walking in His garden for a year prior to the Come to the Garden retreat. I had been living and breathing the garden—praying, studying, and preparing for the garden-themed missions tea and knew that God was doing a deep heart work in me through the garden. But, honestly, I was so focused on all my tasks at hand, including our retreat product table, the missions tea only two weeks later, and a crazy retail schedule, that I gave no thought to what the Lord had in mind for me personally at Come to the Garden. I had no idea that He had so much more for me than the little retreat store He had us create.

On the opening night of Come to the Garden, there was a beautiful time of worship that included singing "What a Beautiful Name." The line of the song that stood out to me was, "Jesus, You brought heaven down." My heart is so tender to heaven now with my boy there—yes, I loved the thought of heaven coming down. But then Edma danced. She danced to "The Garden" song. My song. I was ruined. To describe the eternal depths of everything God did throughout each day and each moment of retreat is beyond words. I bonded with Kayla, one of the FSOD girls who was on the worship team and helped me with some of the set-up and tear down of our retreat store. I would later, after the retreat, "adopt" her as my daughter, and she me as her spiritual mom. The fellowship with the other women was so fun and rich. We walked and talked, ate and shopped together when we weren't in service. While shopping with a group of the girls, I bought a small bangle bracelet that said "NEVER FORGOTTEN" that spoke to me about the loss of my Jordan.

Walking into the sanctuary on Saturday night, I was awestruck by the beauty. Tiffany and her team, capturing Christy's powerful dream that she had been sharing with us during the sessions, had brought the garden into full, glorious bloom. The beauty was breathtaking, and anointing was dripping from every decoration. Here I was seeing the vision for the garden at the missions tea in tangible form—only it was above and beyond what I could think of or imagine. It was the complement, the completion of what God wanted to do in His garden at the missions tea. I watched in wonder as women entered the sanctuary and just stood and soaked in all the sacred beauty.

Once again, during the service, heaven came down. During worship, I had a vision of our store transformed into a garden setting for the next spring's WOW! sessions. I saw it clearly from plants in large pots outside the entrance all the way through the store and to the back with lattice and ivy cascading down the wall. At the end of the service, there was a massive response to the altar call as women were going forward for prayer and going to choose one of the anointed flowers made with a personal word for each of us. Because my grief has been so deep in the loss of my boy, the thought of going to the altar for prayer with someone I didn't know didn't appeal to me. I had been doing my due diligence to seek God's face and heal since the loss of my son, but I just didn't want to do that kind of heart work with a stranger. I just couldn't open up those floodgates publicly. So, I thought I'd just go up and find a quiet place in a corner by myself to get on my face before God. A woman I didn't know at the time came up behind me and began praying. I actually turned and introduced myself and told her that I had lost my son. She began again praying over me, speaking things about the calling on my life and not once, but three times during her prayer she said, "Jordan is NEVER FORGOTTEN." The tears come even again now as I write this. Once again, I was ruined, but clueless about the depths of what God would do the next morning during the closing session.

There's just something about a Sunday—spending a day in His courts is better than a thousand elsewhere. The Sunday at retreat, though, will forever stand as one of the most transforming Lord's Days of my life. It became my Resurrection Sunday. I walked into the sanctuary to see the title of the session on the overhead screens: "Arise, My Love." What? No, it can't be. I could hardly bear it when Edma danced yet again to "The Garden." She danced differently this time, with such victory and thanksgiving and fell to the floor at the end in worship. Christy then began her message by saying, "This is what the Lord gave me today. This is not what I expected," and then she began quoting Isaiah 60: *"Arise, shine, for your light has come, and the glory of the Lord has risen upon you ... "*

You must understand. Isaiah 60:1-4 was the very Scripture the

Lord had given me as the core Scripture to expand the ministry of WOW! before the loss of Jordan. A team had actually been assembled, and we were in the process of walking into that ministry when we lost our son. But all that came to a horrible halt when Jordan left us. While I had come a long way since that horrendous, rainy night of the accident, and I had faithfully continued with the ministry of WOW, I couldn't think of expanding anything. I had stopped dreaming. I actually was afraid to dream again. I was still wearing my grave clothes.

In a message which felt like it was for an audience of one, Christy spoke that Sunday morning. "I believe God has given you a dream, and I believe God's Word to you today is, Arise & Shine." She went on to say, "I believe that God is declaring this morning for you: 'The time of mourning is over. Everything's been buried, and now the time of mourning is over, and He replaces our mourning with garments of praise.'" Hot tears were rolling down my face, but I was unprepared for what would happen next. Christy played the clip from the movie, The Shack, which is about a father's grief journey in the loss of a child. She began the clip of The Shack when the child's casket is being carried into the garden and lowered into the ground. At that point, I felt like King David—nothing mattered in what I needed to do before my King. I couldn't control my weeping. The depths of anguish, the guttural cries that were coming out of me had to come. You see, that very movie had also been my movie. I had watched the ending garden scene over and over and even had saved pictures from it to my iPad. In this ending scene, the father in the movie even has a monarch butterfly land on him—the very thing that God had used to breathe hope into me in the darkest moments of my anguish, just a few short weeks after Jordan left us. I seemed to understand in that moment that although I would grieve and long for my son for the rest of my life, Jordan would be NEVER FORGOTTEN. It was time to shed my grave clothes, step out of the darkness of heavy mourning and back into the fullness of His plan.

Seeing Christy after the session, she had a pained look on her face as I approached her. "Oh, Lisa," she said, "I'm so sorry if I hurt you with showing that clip. The Lord must have blocked you from my mind, otherwise there is no way I would have played that if I had thought of you. I gasped when it started because I suddenly realized what I had done." I told her that she had nothing to apologize about, that actually I felt like she helped launch me.

Home two weeks later, our church had the most beautiful missions tea ever, as the entire gym used for the tea became the garden. Christy and her team donated everything from retreat to be used at the tea and then for us to create the garden in our store. I still didn't quite know how the garden setting I saw in the vision at retreat fit into WOW!, but as I prayed, God resurrected something else that had gotten buried beneath all the grief and sorrow of losing my boy: an online discipleship arm of WOW! called Beautifully Rooted. God had given me the name and format of Beautifully Rooted before losing Jordan. He had even shown me the beautiful logo—an oak tree with WOW! and Beautifully Rooted written along the bottom. Interestingly, in The Shack, a tree miraculously grows in the garden after all of the grieving father's tears that God has collected in a bottle are poured onto the soil. Beautifully Rooted needed a garden to be grown in.

I went on to share everything that had happened at retreat with my leadership team, and we sprung into our WOW! season in the spring by first surprising our staff with a garden party. I knew as I prayed that we needed this garden party to impart the vision for the garden and Beautifully Rooted, as well as to commission them for this ministry season. In addition to the anointed decorations gifted to me from retreat, I was also entrusted with the remaining flowers with the words that I saw God powerfully use to speak so intimately into each woman's life at retreat. When I handed out those holy flowers, I felt like I was being given such a sacred responsibility. As I prayed and God showed me the garden party for our staff, I went back to count the flowers that had been entrusted to me and I discovered I was given eleven—the exact number of our staff. We used one of the altars from retreat and had each of our Trader Rick's family go to the altar to choose their flower after a time of prayer.

We launched Beautifully Rooted at our opening session of WOW! with the store transformed into a gorgeous garden setting dripping with ivy and flowers. We used all the sacred decorations from Come to the Garden, the missions tea, and our garden party. Even the pallet altars from retreat were put into our front windows. Our WOW! attendees enthusiastically embraced Beautifully Rooted, and we already have over 170 women signed up for our online discipleship group. We are doing a year-long garden-themed Bible study, and Beautifully Rooted is drawing women of all backgrounds, from those who have served the Lord for decades, to some who have never before studied the Word of God.

During all of our WOW! sessions, I once again saw women captivated by the beauty of the garden. Our WOW! season was glorious, with women committing their lives to Christ and women putting down deep roots into His living water. Everyone is loving the garden so much that we are leaving it in place through the summer. We know we've only begun to see the blooms and the fruit of all that God wants to grow in His garden.

As for me, as one of the songs sung during the closing session of retreat says, "You called my name, and I ran out of the grave. Out of the darkness into Your glorious day." I miss my son with every breath, but in the resurrection of this mama's broken heart, the Lord breathed life back into me again at retreat. I'm dreaming again, I'm feeling joy again, and I know He has work yet for me to do.

Chapter 12

Flourish, Baby, Flourish

Listen carefully: Unless a grain of wheat is buried in the ground, dead to the world, it is never any more than a grain of wheat. But if it is buried, it sprouts and reproduces itself many times over. In the same way, anyone who holds on to life just as it is destroys that life. But if you let it go, reckless in your love, you'll have it forever, real and eternal.

— John 12:24-25 (MSG)

Seeds. Choice. If I hold the seeds in my hand, they'll always be seeds. But if I bury them in the ground, they become tomatoes, cucumbers, squash, onions and carrots. I have to trust what I can't see happening. If I insist on holding it to watch, the seed will stay a seed, but when I let it go, the seed is transformed. It ceases to be a seed in order that a plant will live. It can no longer find its identity in that of its old self, a seed. It becomes something far different and lives a new kind of life. From the potential of life that is contained within a seed comes a new life capable of producing fruit.

Another interesting thing about a seed is its most obvious feature:

It has a hard outer shell. Now, this hard outer shell has served it's purpose of protection, but it can't grow with the hard shell on. When it's buried and the conditions are right, the seed will draw in moisture, probably river water, and the water will break open the shell. Having served its purpose, the shell is discarded. Some of us have become too friendly with the shell.

If you ask me what is important to me in this life, I can tell you pretty quickly. If we could measure life on the scale of eternity, and you asked me the same question, my answers could be condensed to some of the following: If I was on Twitter, which I'm not, here would be some of my hashtags: #babies #ilovethechurch.

I'm crazy about my kids and my husband. They all think one of the others is my favorite. I have a favorite firstborn. A favorite middle. And a favorite baby. I love the church. I love the vision. I love the adventure of it. I love the people in it. I love to see the can-do volunteer spirit and the selfless spirit of servanthood that strengthens with each generation. I love the music. I love OUR music (since my husband is a Minister of Music). I love to watch people worship, to lose themselves in it. I love the heartbeat, and there can only be one heartbeat. I love to watch God's people champion what is close to His own heart. #comeasyouare #youbelonghere.

"Come as you are" is exactly how Jesus loves us. We live in a day of grace, and the prevailing words over the Gospel invitation of the church to the world should be, "Come as you are; you are welcome here!" Having said that, grace will never leave us as we are, but will always begin a work of transforming us into His likeness. There are no exclusion clauses in heaven's invitation.

All people need to know they belong. A person's color, creed, culture, background, persuasion, sin, or past failings shouldn't exclude them from discovering their personal worth and true personhood in Christ. Sadly, not all professing Christians think like that. I'm not talking about compromising what is scriptural and pure, because the last page in the Bible does say that what is unholy will not enter into heaven. But until that day, Scripture is full of saving grace toward the sinner.

Our commission is to cross every divide with the same compassion that Jesus had and then graciously point people to Him. Redemption is ongoing. So we need to allow God to do the redeeming while we do the loving.

Something worthy to note is that while on earth, Jesus judged only those who displayed an ugly and religious Pharisaic spirit toward others. What is most important in any harvest field is that people see love in action so that they experience it for themselves.

> *Jesus said, 'I am the way and the truth and the life. No one comes to the Father except through Me.'*
>
> — John 14:6 (NIV)

#welcomehome There is a world that needs to hear those words, experience those words and believe those words. I feel a desperation that our church cultures a spiritual wide open and all-embracive welcome mat at every door. To a soul that is void of real love and family, these aren't mere idle words; they're lifeblood. They're words that can introduce people to truth that will in turn nourish their lives and ultimately give them safe passage home, to where they need to be. Home is where we are supposed to flourish, and home is where God does His finest work.

Now, the reality of life is that not every natural or spiritual household is fabulous and lovely or conducive to growth and fruitfulness. Not every home is the garden God would have it to be. So here is an important challenge. We have a very sobering responsibility to make our churches and small groups an environment of life—gardens where God can facilitate His heart toward women and families which will spread and nurture the heart of men and youth and children in a manner that will cause women, men and children to flourish in everything they put their hands to. If we are only flourishing during services, but wilting the other six days of the week, we are missing something.

> *For as the earth bursts with spring wildflowers, and as a garden cascades with blossoms, so the Master, God, brings righteousness into full bloom and puts praise on display before the nations.*
>
> — Isaiah 61:11 (MSG)

God's desire is that our lives flourish in such a stunning manner that they become a display of His goodness before all people. I fully expected the last section to go in a different direction, but the title of that message was "Arise, my love." It was basically a charge. Where you are today. Not tomorrow, not next year, not ten years from now. In your home now. With the people you live with now. In your workplace and schools now. Who you work with now. Arise and shine. Stand up and stand out.

No, not when this lines up and that check comes in and when he leaves. Now. With what and who you have. Now. God wants His glory to shine on you and through you. Now. With what you have. Now. With where you are. Now.

His message to us today is to go home and flourish, baby. I believe that everyone reading this wants to make a difference. I believe everyone reading wants to change the world. He says that if you go forth and flourish, you will. To flourish in your hearts, then flourish in His Word. Go home and flourish in your marriages. Flourish in your parenting. Flourish in your neighborhoods. Flourish in whatever you do.

He says to go home and flourish in your planting. In the place that He has planted you. And if you do, you will change the world. We have seen this happening. It's happening now. It doesn't matter if the garden of your lives is imperfect or even in disrepair. The challenge is to go home and try to make it better.

If your marriage is suffering, God will give you the courage to make whatever adjustments need to be made. If other relationships are in need of attention, God will give you the grace to refresh those relationships. The raw reality is that if the example of our life brings hope and testimony to that of another, enabling them to change, that what we have essentially done is change the world. Being a world changer is insanely possible for all of us. If enough of us were to flourish and excel in our parenting, then raising the next generation of world-class citizens and dynamic leaders would indeed change the world. If enough local churches were to flourish and excel, to become the lighthouses that they are called to be, then communities and our society would change. If enough of us were to flourish and excel in our careers, in our callings, in our God-entrusted gifts, then imagine what would be added to the table. If enough of us were to flourish and excel in compassion and kindness, then the world would be less wounded and broken. And, if enough of us were to flourish and excel in the life-changing Word of God, then imagine the wonder that would be unleashed on this world.

Wherever you are planted in life, you need to know that the soil within that planting is well able to deliver what God has intended and ordained for your life. No soil is perfect. Like everything in life, soil needs to be cared for. It needs to be nourished. It needs to be worked. It needs to be watered. It needs to be rested. And when it is, the seeds of greatness will have a place to take root and eventually emerge.

When we put roots down, we have to be careful to not keep pulling our roots up and moving them around all over the place. We were created to positively contribute wherever God has planted us.

> *The righteous will flourish like the date palm [long-lived, upright and useful]; They will grow like a cedar in Lebanon [majestic and stable]. Planted in the house of the Lord, They will flourish in the courts of our God. [Growing in grace] they will still thrive and bear fruit and prosper in old age; They will flourish and be vital*

and fresh [rich in trust and love and contentment];
[They are living memorials] to declare that the Lord is
upright and faithful [to His promises]; He is my rock,
and there is no unrighteousness in Him.

— Psalm 92:12-15 (AMP)

Most species of palm trees grow in desert climates. They tolerate high temperatures, little rainfall, and high winds. Palms can flourish where other trees would wither and die. God promises that we who serve Him will flourish where others will wither. The circumstances around us will not keep God from providing and will not keep us from thriving.

Palm trees have a different root system than most other trees. Instead of the roots tapering and becoming smaller as they grow farther away from the trunk, palm tree roots stay about the same size. These roots can make their way below the dry, shifting sand to find stability where other trees would not. Our roots are in the Spirit and the Word of God. In a world of fear and insecurity, we have a strong foundation and experience the peace of God.

Unlike most trees that have a woody, dead outer layer, the entire trunk of a palm is alive, allowing it to be very flexible, bending in hurricane-force winds that would break other trees. Storms will come, but God's protection surrounds us, and we will not break. We will come through the storm with victory.

In the Great War of 1914-18 / World War I, red field poppies popped up from the torn, devastated, and battle-scarred landscape of Belgium. In many nations these poppies have become the symbol of remembrance of those who fought and died in this and other wars. God is well able to cause beautiful things to emerge from the most broken and scarred places.

Seeds—if we hold onto them, they're just dry seeds. But when we plant them in the ground, let them go, leave them to God, they flourish. Like my dream, we are called to flourish and salt the earth.

That beautiful garden we read about in Isaiah is finding its full bloom. My prayer is that every generation of ladies, like flowers in a glorious cascading garden, are discovering what it is to be the stunning and magnificent planting of the Lord.

Imagine this world and the people. Imagine nations, cities, and neighborhoods. Imagine the darkened places in public and private places. Imagine the shadows that cloud lives and block out the light. Imagine all that is spiritually and literally stark and barren. But then imagine our homes and our lives in the middle of all the barrenness breaking into glorious color and life.

Imagine your home and your life and all it represents breaking into color. I can only imagine that would resemble an oasis in a dry and thirsty, parched and colorless land. THIS IS WHAT GOD IS AFTER. The ancient prophet Habakkuk said,

> *Look around you . . . among the nations and see! And be astonished! Astounded! For I am putting into effect a work in your days [such] that you would not believe it if it were told to you.*
>
> — Habakkuk 1:5 (AMP)

Let's all take a look around at all that surrounds us. Let's take a good look at where God has us. What needs to be tended to and watered?

> *Listen carefully: Unless a grain of wheat is buried in the ground, dead to the world, it is never any more than a grain of wheat. But if it is buried, it sprouts and reproduces itself many times over. In the same way, anyone who holds on to life just as it is destroys that life. But if you let it go, reckless in your love, you'll have it forever, real and eternal.*
>
> — John 12:24-25 (MSG)

Let's get the seed out of our hand and bury it. If we hold on to it, we destroy the life that is in it. Let's put in the ground where it needs to go. Let it go! Reckless in your love! You'll have it forever, real and eternal. If it's buried, it sprouts and reproduces itself many times over. It's time to flourish!

Chapter 13

Neva

In February 2017, I had an opportunity to attend the Come to the River Women's Retreat in Lake Placid, Florida. Even though I didn't attend the specific host church and had never met these women, I found them to be very loving and welcoming. There was a genuine warmth and loving spirit all around. I felt like I had known them all my life. Amazing! There was such a mighty move of God and tender touch of the Holy Spirit. God was truly using these women to minister to me in a way that I had never experienced before. So, when they announced that they were going to have another retreat in the fall, well, I just couldn't resist attending. I signed up—paid in full!

Throughout that year, the Lord repeatedly impressed upon me to write a book. Since I had never written a book before, this notion seemed to be completely out-of-the-box thinking, for sure. In my mind, I was clearly no author. But that didn't stop the continual pestering. He would frequently remind me of this new direction. It became a daily conversation. The dialog would go something like this: "Really, God? I think You have the wrong person. I'm not equipped to do this, and I don't know what You want me to write about anyway. Surely I must be misunderstanding You." I just couldn't shake it. Surprisingly, there were even times when the topic of writing a book would be mentioned by friends and acquaintances. These comments were completely unsolicited and would appear to have come out of the blue if it hadn't been for the fact that God had been talking to me about it daily.

I prayed for clarity and direction. Then, after months of prayer, He reminded me of my earlier experience at the Come to the River retreat and how the atmosphere there had been filled with His Holy Spirit. Surely these women would help me hear from the Lord and would provide me with some answers.

It was October 2017, at the Come to the Garden Lake Placid Women's Retreat. I had a new purpose for attending. I was focused and determined to understand this new thing God was apparently bringing into my life. So, I decided to go to this event for two specific reasons:

1) To confirm that what I felt was truly the prompting of the Holy Spirit to write a book;

2) To discover what He wanted me to write about.

Much to my surprise, the confirmation to write the book, as well as the topic on which I was to write, were revealed during the Friday night service. That night revealed such a powerful message. The topic was about how God uses the brokenness in the lives of His people to bring about amazing transformation. That He uses the broken things that we experience to strengthen our relationship with Him and creates our testimony to help others. He uses our time of doubt and despair to cultivate greater faith and power in our lives. As the speaker shared, I found myself remembering my past struggles. My mind went back to a time of absolute brokenness, a time when fear and confusion had surrounded and engulfed my heart. It was a season of rebellious choices and selfish desires. It was a time of making desperate decisions to ensure that I could continue to be in control. While I wasn't consciously aware that this was my underlying objective at the time, still, my life's desires were all that mattered. I was willing to remove anything or anyone that got in the way of my life's plans, even the life of my firstborn child. My secret sin was conceived. Oh, what a dark time that was! It was the beginning of years of torment.

Then, as quickly as those discarded feelings flooded my heart, the

Holy Spirit instantly filled my mind with a clear and profound memory of how He totally transformed my life with His healing hand of loving forgiveness. He restored my life. He changed a life that was utterly dying in self-centered rebellion into a life that was alive and gratefully committed to serving others in Christ.

What a revelation! The reminder of my victorious journey took my breath away! It was undoubtedly clear that, while this would not have initially been the topic I would have selected, it was, however, absolutely the subject that He wanted me to write about. He wanted to take my profound brokenness and share it with the hurting and the hopeless. He wanted them to see how, when we place our private brokenness in His hands, He can totally transform our lives. How our lives can become alive with hope and healing, no longer dead in the trappings of sin. He wants all to know that they can truly have a life free from guilt and shame, a life filled with strength and healing for His glory. No sin is too great, too horrible. Oh, what a mighty God we serve!

The following day, during the morning session, there was another moving message given. The topic was about how God repairs our broken vessels in a supernatural way. He doesn't just patch us up. He actually takes pure gold and pours it between our cracks to seal us and make us whole. In the Bible, Peter tells us about such victory over suffering. He explains that it is the very trials in our lives that God uses to show that our faith is real. That the trial itself purifies us just like fire does gold. The fire (trial) causes the impurities (sin) to come to the top so the Master can remove them. This is what refines the gold (hearts) to the most valuable state. So, we can rejoice and find hope when we read; *So be truly glad. There is wonderful joy ahead, even though you have to endure many trials for a little while. These trials will show that your faith is genuine. It is being tested as fire tests and purifies gold—though your faith is far more precious than mere gold. So when your faith remains strong through many trials, it will bring you much praise and glory and honor on the day when Jesus Christ is revealed to the whole world* (1 Peter 1:6-7, NLT). He takes our tested faith to fortify the broken places in our lives.

Our restored lives become of much greater value than before. Remember, God wastes nothing! Even our broken pieces have great value in the Potter's hands. When we place our broken vessel in His hands, we become more valuable than the original pottery because our trials have infused us with gold.

At the end of the speaker's message, an altar call was given. She gave an invitation to those who felt that God was calling them to a higher purpose, a new mission or calling in their lives. The Holy Spirit was at work in me for sure. I couldn't recall, in recent memory, such a pointed, exacting altar call. I began to feel a distinct prompting of the Holy Spirit to respond. I felt an undeniable holy encouragement, a divine direction to go to the altar. I wanted to follow God and the Holy Spirit. I wanted to pledge my willingness to be obedient to His direction. It was during that altar call that this ministry was birthed.

After a magnificent time with the Lord in the altar, I returned to my seat. It wasn't long afterward that I was overwhelmed by what felt like a personal presence of the Holy Spirit. With incredible authority and clarity, He was speaking directly to me. There, sitting at my table, I had a compelling desire to begin to write what He was saying. It seemed like it needed to be documented. He wanted it to be recorded. So, I opened my notebook and took out my pen and started to write.

Now, the truth of the matter is that I really wasn't paying much attention to what I was writing. But I knew I had to write down every word I heard in my heart. The voice in my head was clear and distinct. I didn't take time to review sentence structure or spelling. My focus was just to record what was being revealed. So, I wrote down every word that He gave me, and when He was done, I closed the notebook.

There was a peaceful excitement that surrounded me. I know that sounds like a contradiction. But, honestly, there was such an amazing sensation of resting in His holy presence. A sense like I had ever known before. Never had I felt His presence or experienced Him like that. This was a time of reverence. It felt like holy worship. This was completely new to me. This was something I had only heard about from others. I had never felt this firsthand. Such power! Such clarity! Such direction! I felt like I had left the physical room and entered a special place, a holy place. What was He doing? How should I respond? I was astounded and amazed. I was rendered speechless.

When our morning session ended, I walked back to my room to rest and try to process all that had taken place in the last eighteen hours. There was so much to take in. I had experienced Him privately before. We had shared intimate moments together in my prayer closet. Those times with Him were always wonderful and a real blessing. But this went far beyond anything I could remember. It wasn't a fleeting encounter. It was an ongoing conversation. Everywhere I walked, I heard His voice.

Later that afternoon, while I was taking an afternoon walk, He proceeded to explain to me how He wanted me to write this book. He began to impress upon me the direction I should take. He gave me insights on the spirit I was to convey. Overwhelmed by such precision, I went back to my room. I fell on my face and began to praise God. I cried, wept, laughed at this magnificent encounter, and thanked Him for His profoundly intimate presence. This was far greater than anything I would have ever imagined.

Shortly before dinner, realizing that I hadn't read what I had written earlier, I opened my notebook and proceeded to read. This is what I wrote:

> Trust me to lead you. Remember how I speak to you. Guiding you and your thoughts— impressing your senses to align with my thoughts—says the Holy Spirit. Don't rely on your knowledge, but follow your heart, reveal your past, give God your Testimony, and let me—the Holy Spirit—mold it and use it and form it into the ministry I have for you. You were called back in 1970—in Hermansville, Michigan. That call remains and is strengthened by your life's testimony. Don't be mistaken; I have called you. You are to be my ambassador to help me heal the broken and

bring salvation through their wounding. What the enemy meant for harm, I will use for good. Those children will be the relationship that will bring their parents and loved ones to a deeper relationship with me. Not to separate them from me—that is the enemy's lie. I waste nothing!!! These children are my precious little ones that love and seek me and desire to love and heal their parents from their pain. Like Jesus, God will use their death to bring their parents into my presence—says the Holy Spirit. To be absent from the body is to be present in the Lord. They have been with us (Trinity) from the moment of their death on earth. We have been loving, nurturing, and enjoying them, preparing them for the day of their reunion. We have helped them see you from our eyes. Knowing the lies of the enemy that drew you to make the choice you made, knowing about your fears, confusion, and desperation. Also, about your selfishness, rebellion that consumed you when you made your choice. They have had a Knowing of your life's journeys that would show you the truth and the new life in Christ, the forgiveness of sins and the redemption of lives, knowing that the power of love far exceeds the influence of evil. The children have had excitement and anticipation for this time when you meet again. They have been praying for you with the Father, asking that you would receive the peace of forgiveness. The children cry for you, not out of pain, but out of love for you. They have watched you struggle through the rationalization, justification, and the denial of what happened that day. They understand those tears you shed when the doctor or nurse said, "Don't worry, honey—the tears are normal—it is a hormonal issue." Or when your friend said, "Why are you crying, I thought you wanted to do this?" Your child understood that you just didn't know. Some of the children saw that even though you may have done this with the full knowledge that it wasn't a "tissue" and that they were a human being created by God, you still, at that time, didn't know that the Almighty God designed this to happen. He caught them in their moment and has loved them with a heavenly, holy love because He intended that their life with Him would be the vehicle He was going to use to bring life and salvation to you. Your child's sacrifice, the cost you paid, brought you to the cross to receive eternal salvation.

Wow! As you can see, it was specific and directed. It clearly was not something that I could have made up. As a result, I am following his leading and publishing the book He has called me to write. May you also embrace your healing.

Chapter 9
Stephanie

After sixteen evictions in eleven months, I was quite disillusioned with being a park manager. Twelve of these evictions were people my husband and I had helped to get assistance to move in. I was getting flack from corporate as to why these people weren't vetted more closely before the moves. Why were they allowed to owe so much before evictions were started? It was really making me question my capabilities of doing a good job for the corporation. It was also making me cynical. What excuse is this person going to give me as to why they aren't paying their rent? Why should I believe them that their hours were cut? Are they lying? Are they using drugs? Are they selling them in the park? As people came in to apply to rent or buy a unit, I start asking myself all these questions, including, how long is it going to take this one to cheat us? Or start lying about when they'll pay their rent?

I really needed a break, and I was looking forward to the Come to the Garden Retreat—no whining, no 10:30 p.m. phone calls, but peace and quiet and visiting with friends. I sat back, cynically listening to stories and other people's experiences, trials, and tribulations. My mind was saying, they are here for help, but I'm just here to get a break and have some fellowship. Saturday afternoon, I was given the privilege of explaining to a young lady who was a recovering alcoholic that she was not sick, nothing was wrong, but that she was drunk in the Spirit. God gave me Scripture after Scripture for another friend, to explain to her what she was feeling, what being slain in the Spirit was, and what happens when the power of God comes all over you.

I didn't feel I was there for me, but for others. Those thoughts changed Saturday night. I felt the urge to go forward for prayer, but what good would that do? It wasn't going to change my job. It wasn't going to change my cynical thoughts. Then the light bulb came on; that still, small voice said, "You need to change your heart." I went to Sharon McLaughlin, because I didn't know her, and she didn't know me, and that would stop any embarrassment of mine about needing help, because—I'm not sure what I felt, other than being disillusioned.

When my husband and I had taken the management job over five years previously, we had seen the camp as a continuation of our work with children. I told Sharon I needed a new attitude; I needed compassion again for the people in the park I managed, because I felt I had lost it.

She began to pray, and she said to me, "You are a missionary." After seeing the shocked look on my face, she continued, "Domestic missionaries are just as important as foreign missionaries. God has you right where He wants you. That RV park is your mission field."

I hadn't told her I managed an RV park. My response was, "Thank You, Jesus." I went to pick up a flower, and my word was RELEASED. My verse is Psalm 107:14: *He brought them out of darkness, the utter darkness, and broke away their chains.*

My chains of darkness have been broken. Yes! I felt I was released to minister in my park. I began being bold in ministering from my office. Since Come to the Garden, I have facilitated close to ten first-time salvations and several re-dedications of people coming back to Jesus, as well as praying for many people. I have encountered increased opportunities for counseling and ministering, including performing a wedding in my home. I pray for the strength and energy to do more! Thank you, Christy, for being obedient to God's calling.

Chapter 15
Final Thoughts

"My garden is my most beautiful masterpiece."
—Claude Monet

The Lord will guide you always; he will satisfy your needs in a sun-scorched land and will strengthen your frame. You will be like a well-watered garden, like a spring whose waters never fail.

— Isaiah 58:11 (NIV)

At the last session at our retreat, I played a scene from the movie The Shack. Sarayu takes Mack into the garden at the shack to help her cut flowers and herbs and dig up a tree. He is shocked by the messy lack of order in the garden, but Sarayu tells him that it is actually "a fractal, something considered simple and orderly that is actually composed of repeated patterns."

At the end, Sarayu reveals that the garden they were working on together is actually Mack's soul. Representing Mack's soul as a garden demonstrates how one's life can seem like a complicated series of choices and circumstances, but that what appears as disorder is actually patterns and beauty. Furthermore, by asking Mack to help her uproot a tree, especially one that didn't seem to be causing any problems, to make room for new growth, the author shows how one must accept change as one matures. The work in a garden is never finished. There will always be seasons of tilling up the hard places and removing roots and dead things. There will always be seasons of planting, watering and nourishing. There will always be seasons of waiting. There will always be seasons of growth.

At the first and last session of our retreat we played the song, *The Garden*, by Kari Jobe, while one of our dear ones worshiped with an interpretive dance. It was stunning. And if you knew her own story, you'd understand why it was so stunning. (Her testimony is included in this book.) I want to leave the lyrics of this song with you in closing: It truly sums up our garden experience, my own garden experience, and, I pray, your garden experience through this book.

> ### *The Garden,* by Kari Jobe
> I had all
> But given up
> Desperate for
> A sign from love
> Something good
> Something kind
> Bringing peace to every corner of my mind
> Then I saw the garden
> Hope had come to me
> To sweep away the ashes
> And wake me from my sleep
>
> I realized
> You never left
> And for this moment
> You planned ahead
> That I would see
> Your faithfulness in all of the green

I can see the ivy
Growing through the wall
'Cause You will stop at nothing
To heal my broken soul I can see the ivy
Reaching through the wall
'Cause You will stop at nothing
To heal my broken soul
Ohh, You're healing broken souls
You're healing, You're healing broken souls
Faith is rising up like ivy
Reaching for the light
Hope is stirring deep inside me
Making all things right
Love is lifting me from sorrow
Catching every tear
Dispelling every lie and torment
Crushing all my fears
You crush all my fears
You crush all my fears
With Your perfect love
Oh-ohh, with Your perfect love
Now I see redemption
Growing in the trees
The death and resurrection
In every single seed

Beloved, if you see nothing but barren ground and dead things, the Gardener of your soul wants to remove all things dead and all roots that are choking the life and the joy out of you. He has a future for you that is full of life and blooms and color. He wants to "strengthen your frame." And you will be a like a well-watered garden, like a spring whose waters never fail. Remember how, in real life, I couldn't get anything to grow on my property? I had the dream in February of 2010. By May of 2010, beautiful green grass covered my lawn!

About the author

Christy Sawyer is a minister and teacher of God's word and madly in love with Jesus Christ. Christy is a sought after speaker and teacher for worship services, conferences, and retreats. Through her unique and transparent style of speaking, her primary passion is to point the world to Jesus and to empower men and women to fulfill in their God-given destiny.

In her home church, First Assembly of God in Fort Myers, Florida, she has established a worship and discipleship opportunity just for ladies called "River Dwellers" that meets each Wednesday Night. Over 100 ladies meet to worship, hear the word, and then spend time discussing life applications in small groups.

Christy clings to 1 Corinthians 1:26-29—*Brothers and sisters, think of what you were when you were called. Not many of you were wise by human standards; not many were influential; not many were of noble birth. But, God chose the foolish things of the world to shame the wise; God chose the weak things of the world to shame the strong. God chose the lowly things of this world and the despised things- and the things that are not- to nullify the things that are, so that none may boast before him.*

Christy is married to Reverend Jonathan Sawyer, and they serve in full-time ministry at First Assembly of God, where he is the Worship Pastor. She would love to be a part of an event in your church or group! For booking, email info@christysawyerministries.com.

Notes

Notes

Notes